Orchids of
Minnesota

❧

*The University of Minnesota Press
gratefully acknowledges
the generous assistance provided
for the publication of this book
by the
Margaret W. Harmon Fund
dedicated to the publication of books that promote an
understanding and conservation
of botanical resources
and the
Natural Heritage Program
and
Nongame Wildlife Program
Section of Wildlife
Minnesota Department of Natural Resources.*

Orchids of Minnesota

Welby R. Smith

Natural Heritage Program
Section of Wildlife
Minnesota Department of Natural Resources

Illustrated by
Vera Ming Wong

UNIVERSITY OF MINNESOTA PRESS
Minneapolis   London

Published by the University of Minnesota Press
2037 University Avenue Southeast, Minneapolis, MN 55455-3092

Printed in the United States of America on acid-free paper

Library of Congress Cataloging-in-Publication Data

Smith, Welby R. (Welby Richmond)
    Orchids of Minnesota / Welby R. Smith ; illustrated by Vera Ming Wong.
        p. cm
    Includes bibliographical references and index.
    ISBN 0-8166-2309-0 (hc : alk. paper)
    1. Orchids—Minnesota.   2. Orchids—Minnesota—Identification.
    I. Title.
    QK495.O64S64   1993
    584'. 15' 09776—dc20   92-47478
                                                                                CIP

The University of Minnesota is an equal-opportunity educator and employer.

Contents

ク

Acknowledgments
࿓

I am greatly indebted to the many people whose assistance made this book possible. Among those who contributed materially by providing specimens, locations, or other information are Nancy Sather, Rolf Dahle, Hannah Dunevitz, Lynden Gerdes, Norm Aaseng, Steve Stucker, Roger Lake, Robert Dana, Barb Delaney, Emmet Judziewicz, John Schladweiler, Dick Oehlenschlager, John Moriarty, May Wright, Dennis Hageman, Janet Boe, Donna Sheridan, Fred Harris, Mark Leoschke, Chel Anderson, Audrey Engels, Scott Zager, Faith Campbell, Bill Brumback, John Freudenstein, the Minnesota Orchid Society, and especially Karen Myhre.

Those who contributed to the production of the book include Roleen Roden, Al Epp, B. J. Farley, Tom Klein, John Almendinger, Barbara Coffin, and Judy Melander. Also a special thanks to the following photographers who allowed use of their excellent slides without remuneration: Richard Haug, John Pennoyer, Diane Plunkett, and John Mathisen.

I would also like to thank the curators of the following herbaria for use of their facilities: University of Minnesota, St. Paul; University of Minnesota, Duluth; University of Wisconsin, Madison.

About Orchids

Introduction
ॐ

Orchids in Minnesota?

Orchids are often thought of as rare, fragile objets d'art, existing only in steamy tropical forests or in Edwardian greenhouses. In reality, nothing could be further from the truth. Orchids occur worldwide from the arctic tundra to Tierra del Fuego. They are absent only from the driest deserts and the wettest aquatic habitats. They constitute one of the largest plant families with 725 genera and an estimated 20,000–23,000 species (Atwood, 1986)—that's between 7 and 10 percent of all the flowering plant species on earth (Dressler, 1981).

Although worldwide in distribution, the vast majority of orchids live unnoticed in the tropics and subtropics, where they are epiphytic in the canopies of the tallest trees (an epiphyte being a plant that grows on another plant, but not as a parasite). Relatively few orchid species occur in temperate regions, and all that do are terrestrial (rooted in soil). Actually, one of our more curious bog orchids (*Malaxis paludosa*) may fit the technical definition of an epiphyte. It typically grows perched on top of *Sphagnum* hummocks, and its roots never reach the soil.

Why are there more orchid species in the tropics than in Minnesota? One reason is Minnesota's geological history. Minnesota was covered by glaciers until about 12,000 years ago, which means that all the orchid species now found in the state originated elsewhere and migrated here after the glaciers retreated. To date forty-two species have made the trip. In human terms, this is a rowdy pioneering bunch of orchids that could be called the advance guard or lunatic fringe of orchid evolution. As they compete for a niche in this recently deglaciated landscape (recent in terms of orchid evolution), they are subjected to powerful selective pressures that are the driving force of evolution. The results can be seen in several genera such as *Spiranthes, Goodyera,* and *Platanthera,* which seem to be demonstrating all the stages of speciation before our eyes.

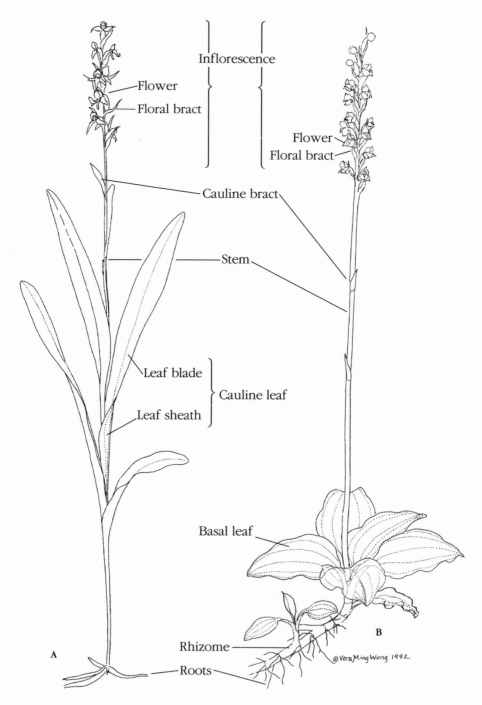

Figure 1. Gross structure of two generalized orchid types: *A—Platanthera*-type orchid, *B—Goodyera*-type orchid

What Makes an Orchid an Orchid?

To understand what makes orchids different from members of other plant families, and from each other, we must first understand how botanists classify plants. Flowering plants, including orchids, are classified largely on the basis of flower structure, and to a lesser degree on inflorescence type, root form, anatomical details, biochemical properties, and cytological features. Those plants with the greatest similarities are assumed to be most closely related and are grouped together.

Some obvious gross features like size, color, leaf shape, and habitat are not used in the classification of plants because they do not actually reflect evolutionary relationships. And yet, such gross features play a dominant role in the cognitive process; we rely on them to visually distinguish one species from another. For example, we can reliably distinguish the *Cypripediums* (lady's-slipper orchids) from all other Minnesota orchids by their distinctive slipper-shaped lip. But what really sets them apart is the fact that they have two fertile anthers instead of the usual one, a detail that is important to understanding evolutionary relationships but not very practical for field identification. By emphasizing gross features, we can construct easy-to-use keys based entirely on superficial but reliable differences.

Orchids share some features with other plant families, such as flowers with three petals and three sepals, leaves with parallel veins, and ovaries inferior to the perianth. Other features are more or less exclusive to orchids and differentiate them from other families (Figures 1 and 2). Perhaps the most unusual feature is the column. This is a single structure formed by the fusion of the stamens and the pistil, and is located at the center of the flower. Another unique structure is the lip or labellum, which is a petal (usually the lowest one) that is modified into a shape or color different from the other petals. Likewise, the dustlike pollen seen in most plants has been modified by orchids into a few large masses called pollinia. Another orchid innovation is a process called resupination, in which the flower actually twists 180° in the normal course of development. The rostellum may be the most curious structure in the orchid flower. It is a modified stigma, and, when present, acts to transfer the pollinia from the anther to the insect pollinator, often with astounding ingenuity. The seeds are also noteworthy in their construction. Not only are they numerous and tiny, but they lack endosperm (stored food) and an organized embryo.

Pollination—Those Clever Orchids

Humans may think that they alone can create art, but only an insect can create an orchid flower. In slightly more scientific terms, orchid flowers exist in their specialized forms only to satisfy the visual and olfactory

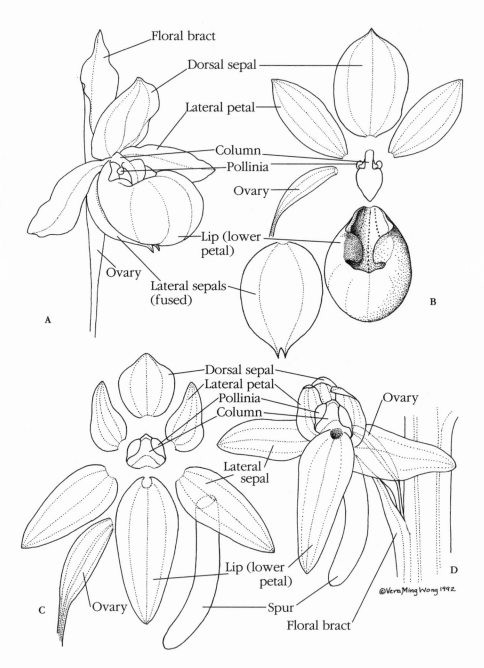

Floral bract
Dorsal sepal
Lateral petal
Column
Pollinia
Ovary
Lip (lower petal)
Ovary
Lateral sepals (fused)

A

B

Dorsal sepal
Lateral petal
Pollinia
Column
Ovary
Lateral sepal
Lip (lower petal)
Ovary
Spur
Floral bract

©Vera Ming Wong 1992

C

D

Figure 2. Floral structure of two generalized orchid types: *A* and *B*—*Cypripedium*-type flower, *C* and *D*—*Platanthera*-type flower

preferences of the insects that pollinate them. In Minnesota, the pollinators are often bees (including bumblebees), moths, butterflies, mosquitoes, gnats, and probably many others. Pollination still has not been observed for several species of native orchids.

In this classical partnership the orchid provides food (or in some cases only the promise of food) and in exchange the insect carries pollen from one flower to another, transferring genetic material and effecting cross-pollination. Examples of the intricate and ingenious relationships resulting from millions of years of coevolution can be seen in several Minnesota orchids.

In the case of the lady's-slippers (*Cypripedium* spp.), bees are attracted by the color and form of the flower as well as by the fragrance that emanates from the lateral petals and sepals (Stoutamire, 1967). The bee lands on the pouch and enters through the opening in the center. It is then temporarily trapped; it cannot get out the same way it got in because of the downward projecting rim around the entrance. After some confusion, the bee is guided by colored lines and long hairs toward one of two small escape openings at the base of the pouch. As the bee approaches the opening the passage narrows, and the dorsal surface of its thorax is forced into contact with the stigma, thereby depositing any pollinia it might have picked up during a previous visit to another lady's-slipper. As the bee finally squeezes out the escape opening it is forced against the anther and picks up the sticky pollinia to be delivered to the next flower it visits. For all its work the bee receives no reward; the plant produces no nectar, and the protein-rich pollen is out of reach on the bee's back. The bee has been fooled, and it eventually learns to avoid similar flowers. But for the pollination process to work the bee must be fooled at least twice: once to pick up the pollinia and once to deliver them.

Some species of orchid take a more active approach to pollination. A good example is *Listera cordata* (heart-leaved twayblade), whose pollination secrets have been worked out in detail by Ackerman and Mesler (1979). The insect pollinator, a fungus gnat or similar-sized creature, is attracted to the flower by a foul odor (described as "truly repulsive" to human senses). The visitor lands on the lip of the flower and reaches for the nectar located directly below the column. In doing so it touches one or more delicately adjusted trigger hairs on the tip of the rostellum (a flaplike piece of tissue covering the stigma). The trap has now been sprung, and a droplet of quick-drying cement is shot from the rostellum onto the pollinator (usually its face). Immediately the margins of the rostellum reflex, forcing the pollinia onto the droplet of wet glue that is already attached to the pollinator. The startled insect retreats, taking the pollinia away to the next flower it visits. About one day after the successful ambush, the rostellum lifts to expose the receptive stigma. Any insect visiting the flower now will encounter the stigma, and if that insect is a previous victim of the "quick-draw" orchid, it will likely be carrying pollinia to deposit, thereby completing the process. If the foul odor seems a strange way to attract insects to an orchid it should be remembered that many insects normally lay their eggs on feces or other decaying organic matter.

Symbiosis—Strange Bedfellows

Insects are not the only organisms that orchids rely upon for survival. A lifelong union is formed between orchids and certain soil-inhabiting fungi. This presumably symbiotic union is termed "mycorrhiza." In this association, the threadlike fungal hyphae enter the orchid through specialized cells on the root or rhizome. Once inside, the contents of the hyphae are expelled by the fungus and digested by the orchid. The orchid obviously benefits from the arrangement, but the benefit to the fungus is unclear.

This relationship between plant and fungus is not unique to orchids. It now appears that most plants, including trees, form mycorrhizal associations. What is unusual is the degree to which orchids have exploited this relationship. Orchid seeds are tiny, often microscopic structures with little if any stored food. Before or shortly after germination fungal hyphae must penetrate the seed and enter the embryo. Without the infusion of nutrients the seed cannot survive. Following the initial stage of germination, the orchid develops into a protocorm and lives entirely underground for up to several years. At this stage it is still entirely dependent on the fungus for its nourishment. When the orchid finally produces aerial shoots and photosynthetic leaves it is capable of producing much of its own food, but the mycorrhizal association may still persist.

Some species of orchid (including our *Corallorhiza*) have taken this symbiosis one step further: they rely entirely on the fungal association during all stages of development. Because the fungus provides all the nourishment, the orchid has no need to photosynthesize, and therefore has little if any chlorophyll, no leaves, and no true roots. Such orchids are usually called saprophytes, meaning that they live on organic matter in the soil. Technically it is the fungus that is saprophytic; it obtains its nutrients by decomposing organic matter, a feat no vascular plant can manage. In this case, the orchid would be a parasite of the fungus, an intriguing reversal of traditional roles. Interestingly, some fungi may form mycorrhizal associations with more than one species at a time, and could act as conduits for nutrients between, for example, an orchid and a tree.

Natural History—How Do Orchids Live?

Minnesota's orchids have a reputation as long-lived denizens of ancient undisturbed forests. But with the possible exception of some *Cypripediums* this is not true. Orchids, like all plants, have evolutionary adaptations for coping with changes in their environment. Some species, notably those in the genera *Spiranthes, Liparis, Corallorhiza,* and to some extent *Platanthera,* seem quite mobile, and are especially well suited to colonize recently disturbed habitats. The evidence for this can be seen in the structure of a typical orchid seed. The seeds are very small, nearly microscopic in size, but as much as 96 percent of the volume is air (Arditti et al., 1979). In this regard they resemble tiny balloons, and can float in the air for great distances—up to 2,000 km (Close et al., 1978) and probably much farther. Adding this to the fact that a single orchid flower can produce an incredible number of seeds (over one million), it is no wonder that orchids are one of the most successful groups of flowering plants.

In spite of the success and the popularity of orchids, questions about their biology far exceed available answers. Very little research has been conducted into even the most basic aspects of their life histories. As a result, surprisingly little is known about how our native orchids live or even about how long they live. For example, we know that the showy lady's-slipper (*Cypripedium reginae*) sometimes occurs in large numbers in coniferous swamps, and there is anecdotal evidence of individual plants living sixty years or longer. But we know next to nothing about its population dynamics, reproductive limitations, habitat requirements, and, perhaps most important, management needs. Likewise, we can describe, but not explain, how some orchids such as the stemless lady's-slipper (*Cypripedium acaule*) can thrive in the driest, sandiest pine forests and also in the wettest *Sphagnum* bogs. We are equally at a loss to explain the apparent boom and bust cycles seen in populations of some species of *Spiranthes, Liparis,* and *Platanthera.* Research possibilities seem endless.

Ecology—Where Can I Find Native Orchids?

Orchids probably occur in every county in Minnesota, and in essentially every terrestrial habitat type. And yet they can be very difficult to find. Even the most common orchids are uncommon when compared to other plants, but this should not discourage anyone who really wants to study native orchids.

For the purpose of discussing orchid ecology in Minnesota, the state can be divided into four major regions, each defined according to the predominant vegetation at the time of European settlement (Figure 3).

The Coniferous Forest Region

This is the largest of the four regions and occupies the northeastern and north central parts of the state. The vegetation at the time of European settlement was characterized by dense forests of coniferous trees, such as pine (*Pinus* spp.), spruce (*Picea* spp.), balsam fir (*Abies balsamea*), cedar (*Thuja occidentalis*), and tamarack (*Larix laricina*). The soils are mostly acidic, and often rocky or saturated. Interspersed within the coniferous

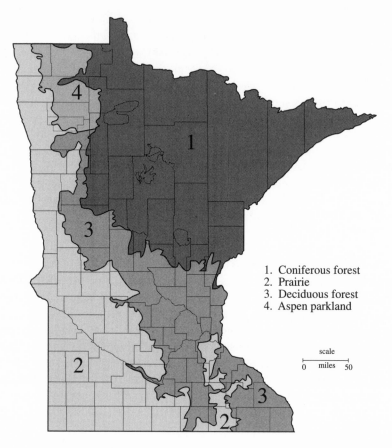

1. Coniferous forest
2. Prairie
3. Deciduous forest
4. Aspen parkland

scale
0   miles   50

Figure 3. Major vegetation types in Minnesota at the time of European settlement (ca. 1850)

forest region were large expanses of nonforested habitats such as muskeg, marshes, and meadows. Completing the mosaic were scattered hardwood stands composed mostly of aspen (*Populus tremuloides*) and paper birch (*Betula papyrifera*), with lesser amounts of red oak (*Quercus rubra*), ash (*Fraxinus* spp.), elm (*Ulmus americana*), maple (*Acer* spp.), and basswood (*Tilia americana*). It was a dynamic landscape subjected to frequent fires.

Although the extent of forest cover in this region has not changed greatly since the time of settlement, the composition and structure of the forest has changed drastically. The best stands of white pine (*Pinus strobus*) and red pine (*Pinus resinosa*) were cut by the 1920s and through natural succession were largely replaced by aspen and birch. Many of these aspen-birch forests are now succeeding to a spruce-fir cover type. However, forestry practices continue to set back succession wherever merchantable timber can be found and harvested. The wetlands in this region have fared somewhat better, with many large areas still surviving in a more or less natural condition. Some of the best places to see remnants of the original vegetation of this region include Scenic State Park near Big Fork and Itasca State Park near Park Rapids.

This region has the largest number of orchids, with at least thirty-four species. Several have boreal affinities and do not occur in any other region. Examples include *Amerorchis rotundifolia* (small round-leaved orchis), *Calypso bulbosa* var. *americana* (fairy slipper), and *Listera auriculata* (auricled twayblade). The greatest concentrations can usually be found in coniferous swamps, especially in a thick mat of *Sphagnum* moss under a canopy of white cedar trees (*Thuja occidentalis*). In this kind of habitat it is possible to find as many as fifteen different orchid species in a few hours of searching.

The Prairie Region

The prairie region is second to the coniferous forest region in geographical extent. Prior to European settlement it was a vast grass-dominated biome interspersed with cattail (*Typha*) marshes and sedge meadows. It was historically maintained by monumental wildfires that regularly swept across the landscape. Occasionally, where a lake or stream formed a natural firebreak, a small relict woodland might survive. The soil is typically calcareous glacial till and very productive. Tragically, very little of the original prairie remains; as much as 99 percent has been converted to agricultural uses, and 90 percent of the wetlands have been drained. Most of the surviving prairies are still vulnerable to land conversion, and even when protected they often suffer from the suppression of wildfires and the invasion of nonnative species. Intact remnants are essentially museum pieces, but they can still be seen at places like Buffalo River State Park near Moorhead and Blue Mounds State Park near Luverne.

About eleven species of orchids can be found in prairies or prairie wetlands, but only three can really be considered prairie specialists: *Cypripedium candidum* (small white lady's-slipper), *Platanthera praeclara* (western prairie fringed-orchid), and *Spiranthes magnicamporum* (Great Plains ladies'-tresses). Because of the loss of prairie habitat *P. praeclara* is listed as endangered in Minnesota (threatened nationally) and *C. candidum* is listed as special concern. *Spiranthes magnicamporum* seems to be more adaptable and probably is secure for the time being.

The Deciduous Forest Region

The deciduous forest region is the next largest in extent and is geographically situated between the prairie and the coniferous forest regions. It is often called a transition zone because it has some prairie influence from the west and coniferous forest influence from the east and north. The main character of this region is provided by fire-sensitive deciduous tree species such as elm (*Ulmus* spp.), red oak (*Quercus rubra*), sugar maple (*Acer saccharum*), and basswood (*Tilia americana*). They originally occurred in large unbroken tracts, which included the "Big Woods" that was so prominent in frontier lore. This region is, in fact, the westward extension of the great eastern deciduous forest that once blanketed the northeastern portion of the United States.

Like that of the prairies, the natural vegetation of this region has been dramatically altered by human activities. At least 90 percent of the original forest cover has been cleared or severely degraded by cattle grazing. Only small "postage-stamp" remnants have been preserved, and these can be seen at such places as Nerstrand Woods State Park near Faribault and Beaver Creek Valley State Park near Caledonia.

As many as thirty-two orchid species have been found in this region. Some are basically northern plants that occur more commonly in the coniferous forest region, but most have southern or eastern affinities and can be found in no other region of the state, including *Aplectrum hyemale* (putty root), *Galearis spectabilis* (showy orchis), and *Liparis lilifolia* (lily-leaved twayblade).

Aspen Parkland

Restricted to the northwestern corner of the state, the aspen parkland is the smallest and most poorly defined of the four regions. Floristically it is most similar to the prairies, but structurally it is a transition between the prairie and the coniferous forest. It is characterized by prairie and wetland vegetation interspersed with groves of fire-tolerant trees such as aspen (*Populus tremuloides*), balsam poplar (*Populus balsamifera*), and burr oak (*Quercus macrocarpa*). There are also large areas dominated by brush, particularly red osier dogwood (*Cornus stolonifera*), willow (*Salix* spp.), dwarf birch (*Betula glandulifera*), and hazel (*Corylus* spp.). Historically it was subjected to wildfires more frequently than the coniferous forests to the east, but less frequently than the prairies to the west; hence the "hybrid" appearance of the landscape.

This region had remained in a comparatively natural state until recently when the high demand for farmland made it profitable to convert the land to the production of cash crops. The suppression of wildfires has also changed the appearance of the landscape, allowing prairies to succeed to brushland and brushland to succeed to woodland. A glimpse of the original character of this region can be seen at Lake Bronson State Park near Karlstad and at Twin Lakes Wildlife Management Area, also near Karlstad.

Only five species of orchid have been found in this region, and none occurs here exclusively. The orchids that do occur in this region are quite abundant here and are commonly seen even in the roadside ditches. This is especially true of *Cypripedium reginae* (showy lady's-slipper), both varieties of *C. calceolus* (yellow lady's-slipper), and *Spiranthes romanzoffiana* (hooded ladies'-tresses).

Conservation—The Future of Our Native Orchids

It is not a pleasant thought, but the orchids we enjoy so much today may be gone tomorrow. Orchid habitats statewide have been reduced by perhaps 75 percent. Many habitats like prairies and old growth forests have been reduced by as much as 95 percent, and the losses are continuing. The changes have been truly profound, but still many people, especially metropolitan residents, are only vaguely aware of what has been lost. It always comes as a surprise to hear that until early this century a tamarack swamp on the shore of Lake Calhoun in the heart of Minneapolis had large populations of *Cypripedium acaule* (stemless lady's-slipper), *C. calceolus* var. *parviflorum* (small yellow lady's-slipper), and *C. reginae* (showy lady's-slipper). Likewise, *Spiranthes cernua* (nodding ladies'-tresses) could be found on the shores of Como Lake in St. Paul; *Coeloglossum viride* var. *virescens* (long-bracted orchid) and *Galearis spectabilis* (showy orchis) were common in the glens of Minnehaha Park; and *Calopogon tuberosus* (grass-pink), *Platanthera flava* (tubercled rein-orchid), and *P. praeclara* (western prairie fringed-orchid) were abundant in meadows at Fort Snelling. All of these habitats are gone now.

The loss of habitats in the agricultural region has been even more dramatic. For example, late in the nineteenth century *Platanthera praeclara* (western prairie fringed-orchid) was described as "abundant" in the Minnesota River drainage (MacMillan, 1892). That area is in the heart of the orchid's range and encompassed over 15,000 square miles of prime prairie habitat. Today less than 1 percent of the prairie remains, and the orchid has not been seen there since 1939. It is now listed as endangered, but whatever protection that affords may be too little and too late.

Our native orchids, and indeed all our native plants, are in a steep decline. Loss of habitat through agriculture, forestry, mining, and urban development is the primary cause, but even where habitat can be protected orchids still face the threat of species-specific exploitation. Stories abound of unscrupulous nursery workers removing truckloads of yellow lady's-slippers from the forests around Lake Minnetonka, and of local high-school boys being recruited to dig orchids en masse in our northern forests. These orchids often end up in reputable nurseries under the misleading label of "nursery propagated," which means only that they have been held in the nursery for a minimum of one growing season.

Terrestrial orchids are nearly impossible to propagate artificially. There has been some recent success with tissue culturing *Cypripedium reginae* (showy lady's-slipper), but survival is poor. Likewise, it is possible to propagate *C. calceolus* (yellow lady's-slipper) and *C. acaule* (stemless lady's-slipper) through division, but the process is so slow that it is commercially unviable (Brumback, 1990). As a result, essentially all of the native orchids that are sold commercially are taken from the wild. What makes the situation even more tragic is that nearly all of them will die within a few years. They are really unsuited for gardens and should be left in the wild. This caution also applies to the individual who may be tempted to transplant an orchid from the wild into a garden—please think twice.

State laws designed to protect native orchids as well as other vulnerable species include M.S. 17.23, conservation of certain wildflowers; M.S. 84.0895, protection of threatened and endangered species; and various trespass laws. Unfortunately, these laws are difficult to enforce and only the most flagrant abuses are prosecuted. In the end only public opinion will bring about change. And public opinion is changing, thanks in part to organizations such as the Minnesota Native Plant Society and the Minnesota Orchid Society, who strongly oppose taking native plants from the wild for commercial or horticultural purposes.

Even practitioners of the benign art of photography must take responsibility for the impact they have on their orchid subjects. Remember to tread lightly, especially in bog and swamp habitats, and to refrain from significantly altering the habitat to improve a picture.

How to Use This Book

This book approaches the study of orchids from three directions: identification, distribution, and ecology. The first step is usually identification, which is accomplished by the use of dichotomous keys. Each key offers a succession of paired choices or dichotomies. For each pair, one of the choices will more accurately describe the specimen in question, and will lead to the next pair of choices. Making the correct choice may involve close examination and careful measurement of small features. This will require a measuring scale with increments of 1 mm or smaller, and magnification of at least 5X. A hand lens is usually adequate, but a dissecting microscope is ideal. To avoid mistakes, it is important to read both choices carefully and to interpret them literally.

The descriptions are meant to augment the keys by describing in more detail the normal range of variability seen in our local populations. Extreme or abnormal specimens can be found in many populations, but beginners must learn to avoid them when using the keys. Likewise, the drawings can be very useful for comparison with unknown specimens, but no single illustration can possibly show the full range of variability seen in nature.

Inevitably, some orchids will prove difficult to identify, especially those in the genera *Spiranthes* and *Goodyera.* But don't be discouraged: it is possible to learn to recognize all of the orchids on sight.

The Minnesota distribution maps are based on herbarium specimens that have been seen and verified by the author. Each dot represents the location where a specimen was collected; open dots are specimens collected before 1950, solid dots are specimens collected from 1950 to 1992 (see back endleaf for county map). The maps are intended mostly for general interest, but they also contain a wealth of information relating to plant geography, ecology, glacial history, and more. Analyzing the various patterns of distribution could in itself form the basis of a lifelong study.

The North American range maps were prepared from a variety of published sources, such as monographs, state floras, checklists, and so on. But because of the geographical data gaps in the literature, as well as conflicting taxonomic treatments, the accuracy of the final maps may vary. This should not detract from the main purpose of the maps, which is to present the Minnesota distributions in a broader context.

The phenology and habitat descriptions are based on information from herbarium labels and from direct observations. As such, they represent our current state of knowledge, which is incomplete at best. It is hoped that any inadequacies will be forgiven, or, better yet, taken as a challenge to further our knowledge about native orchids.

Illustrated Key

Illustrated Key to the Genera of Orchids Occurring in Minnesota
🌿

1. Leaves basal or absent at flowering time, the stem bearing at most only vestigial bractlike leaves.

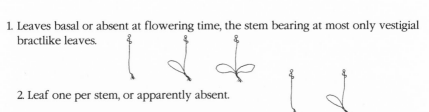

2. Leaf one per stem, or apparently absent.

   3. Leaves entirely absent, or at least withered and dying by the time the flowers appear.

      4. Flowers uniformly white, spirally arranged in a dense spikelike raceme.

                                     Spiranthes magnicamporum, page 153

      4. Flowers variously colored but not uniformly white, not in an obvious spiral or dense spikelike raceme.

         5. Flower one per stem, perianth at least 2 cm long, lip with a crest of fleshy yellow bristles.

                                    Arethusa bulbosa, page 37

         5. Flowers two or more per stem (usually several), perianth less than 2 cm long, lip without a crest.

            6. Stem arising from a globular corm; leaf ovate, arising directly from the corm, usually withered by the time the flowers appear but fragments can often be found.

                                     Aplectrum hyemale, page 33

            6. Stem arising from a much-branched coralloid rhizome; leaves never produced.

                                       Corallorhiza, page 51

3. Leaf present at flowering time, not withered or dying.

   7. Floral lip producing a distinct spur at base (at least 4.5 mm long).

      8. Flowers white with purplish markings; lip three-lobed; leaf elliptical (widest at the middle).

      Amerorchis rotundifolia, page 29

      8. Flowers a uniform greenish color, lip entire; leaf obovate (widest above the middle).

      Platanthera obtusata, page 133

   7. Lip without a spur.

      9. Flower one per stem; leaf ovate, not more than three times longer than wide.

      Calypso bulbosa var. *americana*, page 45

      9. Flowers two or more per stem; leaf linear and grasslike, at least six times longer than wide.

      Calopogon tuberosus, page 41

2. Leaves two or more per stem.

   10. Floral lip formed into an inflated pouch or "slipper" 3.3–6.0 cm long.

   Cypripedium acaule, page 67

   10. Lip not an inflated pouch (although saccate in *Goodyera*), less than 2.0 cm long.

      11. Lip producing a distinct spur at base (at least 5 mm long).

12. Sepals and petals greenish, yellowish, or whitish, wide-spreading; stems 20–60 cm long (including inflorescence); lip no more than 5 mm wide; inflorescence usually more than 8 cm long and consisting of more than ten flowers.

Platanthera, page 117

12. Sepals and petals purple, connivent to form a hood arching over the column; stem 8–25 cm long (including inflorescence); lip at least 6.5 mm wide; inflorescence usually less than 8 cm long and with fewer than ten flowers.

Galearis spectabilis, page 81

11. Lip without a spur.

13. Flowers uniformly white; stem arising from a horizontal rhizome or from a fascicle of thick fleshy roots.

14. Floral lip saccate; stem from a creeping horizontal rhizome, densely pubescent; flowers not typically spiraled.

Goodyera, page 83

14. Lip not saccate, more or less flat with wavy margins; stem from a fascicle of thick fleshy roots, glabrous or pubescent on only the upper half; flowers usually in a spiraled pattern.

Spiranthes, page 146

13. Flowers greenish or purplish; stem arising from a pseudobulb.

15. Flowers minute, the perianth never more than 3 mm long; leaves two to five per stem, less than 2 cm long; floral lip widest below the middle; pseudobulbs of successive years arranged one on top of another.

Malaxis paludosa, page 113

15. Flowers relatively small but not minute, the perianth at least 4 mm long; leaves two per stem, more than 3 cm long; floral lip widest above the middle, pseudobulbs arranged side by side.

Liparis, page 93

1. Leaves not basal, stem with one or more fully developed leaves borne above the base of the stem.

16. Leaves one or two per stem; when two then opposite.

17. Floral lip producing a distinct spur at base (about 1 cm long).

Platanthera clavellata, page 121

17. Lip without a spur.

18. Leaves two, opposite.

Listera, page 99

18. Leaf one.

19. Flowers several per stem, greenish or whitish, minute, the perianth less than 3 mm long.

Malaxis, page 109

19. Flowers one per stem, pink to purple, the perianth more than 1 cm long.

Pogonia ophioglossoides, page 143

16. Leaves three or more per stem, alternate.

20. Floral lip formed into an inflated pouch or "slipper"; spur absent.

Cypripedium, page 63

20. Lip flat, not an inflated pouch; a distinct spur produced at base of lip.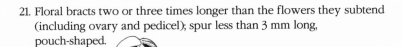

21. Floral bracts two or three times longer than the flowers they subtend (including ovary and pedicel); spur less than 3 mm long, pouch-shaped.

Coeloglossum viride var. *virescens*, page 49

21. Floral bracts usually less than twice as long as the flowers; spur more than 3 mm long, elongate.

Platanthera , page 117

Species Accounts

The Genus Amerorchis *Hultén*
୬ৎ

The name *Amerorchis* distinguishes this as an American version of the Old World genus *orchis*, a Greek word meaning testicle.

Historically included in the large and often ill defined genus *orchis*, but lacking the tuberoids of that genus. As currently defined, *Amerorchis* constitutes a monotypic genus endemic to arctic and boreal North America.

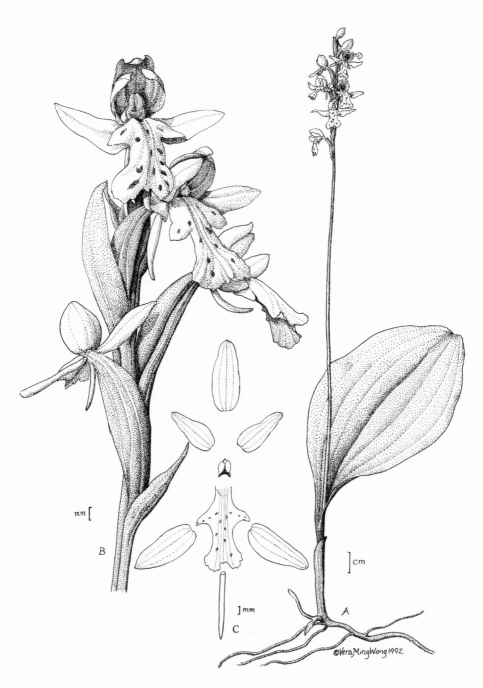

Amerorchis rotundifolia ***A***–Flowering plant, ***B***–Portion of inflorescence, ***C***–
Flower, exploded view

Amerorchis rotundifolia (Banks) Hultén

Synonym: *Orchis rotundifolia* Banks ex Pursh.

Common name: Small round-leaved orchis.

Abundance: Locally common in parts of northwestern and north central Minnesota; occasional or even rare elsewhere in the state.

Habitat: In a variety of coniferous swamps, usually under a canopy of cedar (*Thuja*), tamarack (*Larix*), or spruce (*Picea*). Preferring a substrate of deep *Sphagnum.*

Known flowering dates: June 5-July 22.

Description: Stem 15-36 cm long (including inflorescence), glabrous; roots few, from a

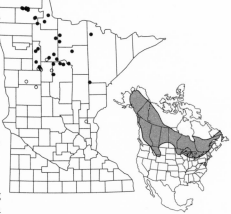

slender rhizome; leaf one, essentially basal, subtended by one or two bladeless sheaths, elliptical, obtuse, 5-15 cm long, 2.0-8.5 cm wide; inflorescence a terminal raceme 3-13 cm long (usually less than 6 cm), consisting of 4 to 18 flowers; floral bracts lanceolate, 4-20 mm long; ovaries 7-13 mm long, 1.0-1.5 mm wide at anthesis; sepals white to pale pink, ovate, 5.0-8.0 mm long, 1.7-4.2 mm wide; petals whitish to pink or purplish, ovate, connivent with dorsal sepal to form a vague hood over the column, 4.5-7.0 mm long, 1.5-2.7 mm wide; lip white, spotted with purple, three-lobed, the terminal lobe much larger than the lateral lobes and itself somewhat two-lobed, 6.5-10.0 mm long, 4.0-7.5 mm wide across the lateral lobes; spur about 5 mm long.

Aid to identification: Most likely to be confused with the common *Platanthera obtusata.* Both are rather small swamp orchids with a short inflorescence and a single basal leaf. The flowers of *P. obtusata*, however, are a uniform greenish yellow color, and the leaf is obovate (widest above the middle). The flowers of *Amerorchis rotundifolia* are white with pink or purple markings, and the leaf is elliptical (widest at the middle). Also, the floral lip of *P. obtusata* is entire, and the lip of *A. rotundifolia* is three-lobed.

A pure white form (f. *beckettae* Boivin) is known, as is a form in which the purplish spots on the lip are replaced by two broad purplish strips (f. *lineata* (Mousley) Voss).

Comments: This much sought after orchid has acquired a questionable reputation for being rare. It is true that you cannot expect to find it while remaining within sight of your car, but there are still substantial populations in every large peatland complex in northwestern and north central Minnesota. It can also be found, but with less regularity, in the smaller, more isolated swamps within the coniferous forest region.

The Genus Aplectrum *Nutt.*

❧

The name *Aplectrum* is from the Greek word meaning "without spur," in reference to the flowers.

A small genus consisting of two species, one in Japan and one in eastern North America.

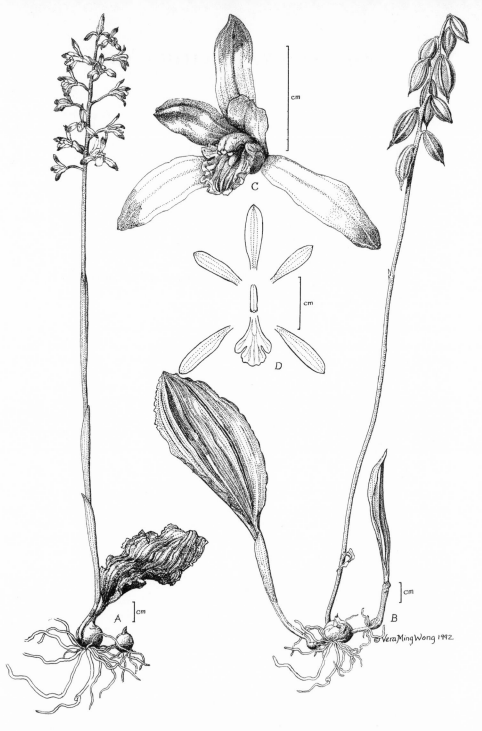

Aplectrum hyemale ***A***—Flowering plant with withered leaf from previous season, ***B***—Fruiting plant, with leaves of current season, ***C***—Flower, ***D***—Flower, exploded view

Aplectrum hyemale (Muhl. ex Willd.) Nutt.

Common name: Putty root.

Abundance: Occasional to frequent.

Habitat: Mesic deciduous forests of the type usually dominated by sugar maple (*Acer saccharum*), basswood (*Tilia americana*), elm (*Ulmus*), or red oak (*Quercus rubra*). Probably most abundant in the calcareous soils of the "Big Woods," but also in the more acidic soils of the Paleozoic Plateau.

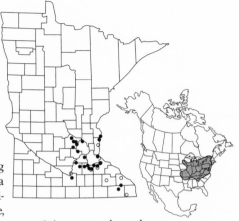

Known flowering dates: May 27-June 16.

Description: Stem 25-44 cm long (including the inflorescence), glabrous, arising from a more or less globular corm 1.5-3.0 cm in diameter; roots numerous, fibrous; leaf one, emerging directly from the corm in autumn remaining green throughout the winter and withering as the plant approaches anthesis the next spring, ellipti-calal to obovate, the blade 8-15 cm long, 2-7 cm wide, dark green with numerous parallel white veins, longitudinally pleated, petiole 3.5-10.0 cm long; inflorescence a terminal raceme 4-12 cm long, consisting of 6 to 16 flowers; floral bracts lanceolate, 2-6 mm long; ovaries 7-14 mm long, about 1 mm wide at anthesis; sepals oblanceolate to oblong-spatulate, greenish tinged with purple toward the tip, 9.0-12.0 mm long, 1.2-3.5 mm wide; petals similar to sepal but somewhat smaller; lip whitish marked with purple, obovate, with a lateral lobe on each side near the middle, crenulate on the apical margin, 7.5-11.0 mm long, 5.0-6.5 mm wide at the widest point, spur absent.

Aid to identification: The flowering stem resembles *Corallorhiza* in that it has no apparent leaf and very little green color. The fruiting stem also resembles *Corallorhiza* in its pendant capsules. *Aplectrum* differs in having a globular corm instead of a branching coralloid rhizome. For much of the year (spring and autumn) *Aplectrum* is visible only as a single sterile leaf, and may not give the impression of an orchid at all. The appearance of the leaf is unmistakable: it has numerous white, parallel veins on a dark green background and a pleated, papery texture that brings to mind a Japanese fan.

Comments: The single leaf of *Aplectrum* is present only in the autumn, winter, and early spring when the canopy trees are bare and enough sunlight reaches the forest floor for net photosynthesis to occur (Auclair, 1972). During early summer the forest floor is too dark to allow efficient photosynthesis, but competition for pollinators is presumably less, so the leaf is abandoned and a nonphotosynthetic flowering shoot appears.

The sterile leaves are often found in dense colonies 2 or 3 meters across and may contain a hundred or more individuals, but few (often only one or two) produce flowers in any given year.

Reported to be pollinated by small bees of the family *Halictidae* (Hogan, 1983).

The Genus Arethusa *L.*

The name *Arethusa* is after the river nymph of classical Greek mythology.

A genus consisting of a single species (*A. bulbosa*) endemic to boreal and north-temperate parts of eastern North America. A similar and possibly congeneric species (*Eleorchis japonica*) occurs in Japan.

Arethusa bulbosa **A**–Flowering plant, **B**–Fruiting plant, showing elongated leaf, **C**–Flower, **D**–Flower, exploded view

Arethusa bulbosa L.

Common name: Dragon's-mouth.

Abundance: Occasional to infrequent.

Habitat: In coniferous swamps of all types, but typically on a substrate of deep *Sphagnum* moss under partial canopy gaps. Also on floating mats around "bog" lakes and in peaty, acidic sedge meadows.

Known flowering dates: May 23-July 23.

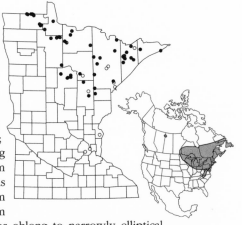

Description: Stem 7-36 cm long, glabrous; roots few, fibrous, from a bulbous corm; leaf one, linear lanceolate, bractlike during anthesis and later extending up to 18 cm long, 3-8 mm wide, 2 to 4 bladeless sheaths below; flower one; floral bract 2-4 mm long; ovary 8.0-10.0 mm long, 1.0-4.0 mm wide at anthesis; sepals rose-purple, linear oblong to narrowly elliptical, 2.5-4.5 cm long, 4.5-8.0 mm wide; petals similar to sepals but somewhat shorter and proportionately wider, connivent and forming a vague hood over the column; lip pink with rose-purple markings, oblong, curving downward near the middle, margins crenulate-erose on upper half, with a crest of fleshy yellow bristles, 2.6-3.8 cm long, 0.6-1.5 cm wide near the apex.

Aid to identification: The single brilliant rose-purple flower and the apparent absence of leaves at anthesis are good field characters for tentative identification. *Pogonia ophioglossoides* and *Calypso bulbosa* var. *americana* also have a single flower with similar colors and a crest of fleshy yellow bristles on the lip, but they both have an obvious leaf at anthesis. In *Arethusa* the leaf begins to elongate only after the flower withers, eventually becoming up to 18 cm long and appearing somewhat grasslike.

A white-flowered form (f. *albiflora* Rand & Redfield) and a lavender-flowered form (f. *subcaerulea* Rand & Redfield) have been described; although very rare, either one or both could be found in any population of normal-colored plants.

Comments: This elusive orchid has a reputation for being rare and occurring in small isolated colonies. But where large expanses of suitable habitat exist, as in the patterned peatland complexes of northern Minnesota, populations often extend unbroken over several square miles and individuals number in the tens of thousands. In fact, Minnesota may be a stronghold of this species, as one of the few areas west of the Canadian Maritime Provinces where *A. bulbosa* appears to be holding its own against the various assaults of humankind (which is not to say that losses of the species have not occurred or will not continue to occur in this region).

Reported to be pollinated only by queen bumblebees, which are attracted by the bright yellow bristles on the lip that are thought to mimic pollen-filled anthers (Thien and Marcks, 1972).

The Genus Calopogon *R. Br.*

The name *Calopogon* is from the Greek words meaning "beautiful beard," in obvious reference to the yellow-tipped bristles on the lip.

A small genus of four species, all endemic to North America. Three occur only in the southeastern states; the fourth occurs over a large portion of the eastern United States and Canada, including Minnesota.

Calopogon tuberosus **A**–Flowering plant, **B**–Inflorescence (with three flowers), **C**–Flower, exploded view

Calopogon tuberosus (L.) BSP.

Synonym: *Calopogon pulchellus* (Salisb.) R. Br.

Common name: Grass-pink.

Abundance: Occasional to frequent.

Habitat: A variety of coniferous swamps, usually under a sparse canopy of spruce (*Picea*), cedar (*Thuja*), or tamarack (*Larix*). It also occurs on floating mats dominated by sedges or *Sphagnum* moss.

Known flowering dates: June 18-August 3.

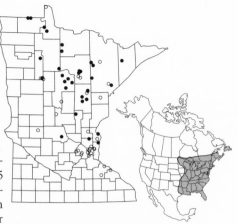

Description: Stem 19-55 cm long, glabrous, arising from a bulbous corm; leaf one, essentially basal, linear, and grasslike, 10-35 cm long, 0.2-1.6 cm wide; inflorescence a terminal raceme, 3.0-13.0 cm long, 2.0-5.5 cm wide, consisting of 2 to 12 pink to purple or rarely white flowers, floral bracts ovate-lanceolate, 4-8 mm long; ovaries 7-10 mm long, 1-2 mm wide at anthesis; sepals ovate to oblong or elliptical, 1.2-2.4 cm long, 5.0-11.0 mm wide; petals oblong or oblong-elliptical 1.3-2.4 cm long, 5.0-8.5 mm wide; lip uppermost of the floral parts (flower not resupinate), broadly "winged" at the apex, and somewhat dilated at the base, 1.1-2.0 cm long, 6.5-14.0 mm wide at the widest point, bearded on ventral surface with clavate yellow-tipped bristles; column incurved, broadly winged at apex, 1.1-1.7 cm long, 6.0-9.0 mm wide.

Aid to identification: The most distinctive features of this species include the single long grasslike leaf that is attached at the base of the stem, and the raceme of two or more relatively large pink to purple flowers. *Arethusa bulbosa* has a single narrow leaf, but only one flower. *Pogonia ophioglossoides* is also similar in having a single relatively narrow leaf, but the leaf is attached nearly halfway up the stem, not at the base, and it typically has just one flower. *Calopogon* is the only one of the three in which the flower is not resupinate. As a result the lip appears at the top of the flower instead of the bottom. White-flowered individuals (f. *albiflorus* Britton) have been found but are vey rare.

Comments: The yellow-tipped bristles on the lip apparently mimic pollen-filled anthers, which attract small bees. The lip is hinged at the base, so when the bee lands, the lip suddenly bends downward. This action throws the bee onto the column, forcing it into contact with the stigma, and depositing any pollinia it might have picked up from another flower. As the confused bee leaves, it picks up new pollinia to be delivered to the next flower it visits (Thien and Marcks, 1972).

The Genus Calypso *Salisb.*

The name *Calypso* is in honor of the mythical sea nymph of Homer's *Odyssey,* and means "hiding" or "concealment."

A distinctive genus consisting of a single wide-ranging species (*C. bulbosa* (L.) Oakes) with four described varieties, one of which occurs in Minnesota.

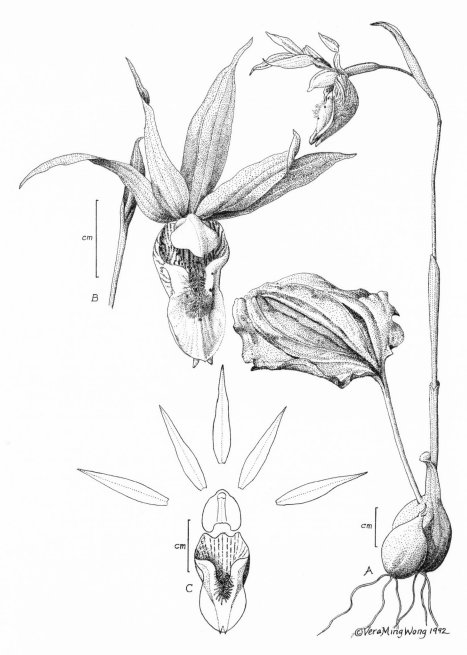

Calypso bulbosa var. *americana* **A**–Flowering plant, **B**–Flower, **C**–Flower, exploded view

Calypso bulbosa (L.) Oakes var. *americana* (R. Br.) Luer

Common name: Fairy slipper.

Abundance: Occasional to infrequent.

Habitat: Most often in lowland conifer- ous forests, particularly under cedar (*Thuja*), spruce (*Picea*), and fir (*Abies*). It typically chooses a substrate of coarse woody humus rather than saturated peat or deep *Sphagnum*. It occurs to a lesser ex- tent in upland coniferous forests, espe- cially in needle duff under pines.

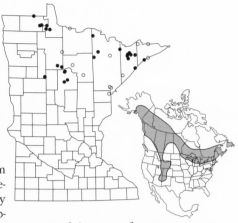

Known flowering dates: May 28-June 22.

Description: Stem one, rarely two, 6-21 cm long, with two or three overlapping blade- less sheaths on lower half; roots two, rarely three, produced from the base of an ellip- soid to ovoid corm; leaf one, arising from the summit of the corm after an- thesis, overwintering, ovate, blade 2.9-5.5 cm long, 1.7-3.3 cm wide, petiole 1-5 cm long; inflorescence a single nodding flower; floral bract lanceolate, 8-14 mm long; ovary pedicellate, curved, 4.0-7.5 mm long, 1.0-2.2 mm wide at anthesis; sepals and petals similar, spreading, purplish to pink, lance-linear, 1.3-2.2 cm long, 2.5-4.5 mm wide at the widest point; lip white to pink, streaked with purple, saccate, ovate to oblong, 1.4-2.2 cm long, 6.0-11.0 mm wide, with two small horns or teeth at the tip, margin expanded forward to form a whitish apron with a crest of yellow bristles; column petaloid, suborbicular, more or less covering the opening of the "slipper."

Aid to identification: *Calypso bulbosa* var. *americana* is best characterized by its single ovate leaf, which arises directly from the corm, and by its intricate and color- ful flower. The leaf is produced in the fall, and remains green through the winter. When the snow melts in the spring the leaf is immediately visible, although by no means conspicuous. At this stage few people would recognize it as an orchid. In late May or early June the distinctive flower emerges and its identity becomes obvious. By late summer the capsule has ripened and the seeds are dispersed. Soon the leaf withers and the plant becomes dormant until September, when the new leaf is pro- duced. *Arethusa bulbosa* is perhaps the closest in appearance to *Calypso*, but re- semblance is vague at best.

The white-flowered f. *candida* Hylander has been found in St. Louis County, and probably occurs elsewhere as well.

Comments: Of all our orchids *Calypso* is perhaps the one most closely associated with the pristine qualities of the northern wilderness. It is a singular and elusive or- chid that cannot be found on demand. It seems to be short-lived and somewhat ephemeral, which may explain its romantic and mythical reputation.

At least ten species of bumblebees have been identified as pollinators of *Calypso* (Mosquin, 1970; Boyden, 1982).

The Genus Coeloglossum *Hartm.*

❧

The name *Coeloglossum* is from the Greek words meaning "hollow tongue," in reference to the shape of the spur.

For many years American botanists have included *Coeloglossum* in the large genus *Habenaria*, but the current trend is to consider *Coeloglossum* a distinct genus consisting of a single polymorphic species, *C. viride*, with several described varieties occurring across North America, Europe, and Asia. One variety, *C. viride* var. *virescens*, occurs in Minnesota.

Coeloglossum viride var. *virescens* **A**–Flowering plant, **B**–Portion of inflorescence, **C**–Flower, exploded view

Coeloglossum viride (L.) Hartm. var. *virescens* (Muhl.) Luer

Synonym: *Habenaria viridis* (L.) R. Br. var. *bracteata* (Muhl.) Gray.

Common name: Long-bracted orchid.

Abundance: Occasional to locally frequent.

Habitat: In a wide range of upland forest types, preferring mesic hardwoods but also under pine (*Pinus*), spruce (*Picea*), and fir (*Abies*). Typically in full shade and in well-drained acidic soil.

Known flowering dates: May 20-August 9. The flowers persist for some weeks after pollination.

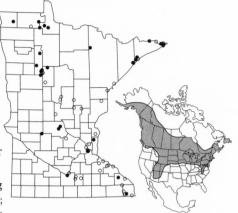

Description: Stem 14-53 cm long (including inflorescence), glabrous; roots few, fleshy; leaves cauline, the middle and lower ones elliptical to oblong or obovate, rather blunt, the upper leaves lanceolate, resembling the floral bracts but larger, 2 to 6 per stem with 1 to 4 bladeless sheaths below, 5.0-13.0 cm long; 0.8-6.5 cm wide, inflorescence a terminal spicate raceme, 4.5-24.0 cm long, consisting of 11 to 76 greenish flowers; floral bracts lanceolate, foliaceous, 1.0-5.5 cm long, 0.3-1.2 cm wide near the base, the lower ones two to three times longer than the flowers; ovaries 4.5-8.0 mm long, 1.2-2.0 mm wide; dorsal sepal broadly ovate to nearly elliptical, 3.0-5.5 mm long, 1.7-3.0 mm wide; lateral sepals ovate, oblique, 4.2-7.0 mm long, 2.0-4.0 mm wide; petals linear to lance-linear, 3.5-4.5 mm long, about 0.6 mm wide; lip oblong or strap-shaped, the apex truncate with two long blunt parallel teeth, 4.0-11.0 mm long, 0.8-3.5 mm wide; spur pouch-shaped, 2.0-2.7 mm long.

Aid to identification: It is easy to mistake this species for *Platanthera hyperborea* or *P. flava*, especially in the field. The floral bracts of *C. viride* var. *virescens* are characteristically longer, with the lower ones usually over 3 cm long, and two to three times longer than the flower (including ovary and pedicel). In any similar-looking *Platanthera* the bracts are well under 3 cm in length, and less than twice as long as the flower. Also, the spur of *C. viride* var. *virescens* is much shorter than in any of our *Platantheras* (generally no more than 2.5 mm long), and the long teeth or "tusks" at the apex of the lip are also unique.

Comments: This interesting orchid is widespread in Minnesota, but it is little studied and little appreciated. As a result there are large gaps in our knowledge, especially relating to distribution and ecology. It appears that *C. viride* var. *virescens* could be found in nearly any mesic forest habitat in Minnesota, but it is probably most frequent in the hardwood transition zone that runs southeast to northwest from Houston County to Kittson County.

The Genus Corallorhiza *(Hall.) Chat.*
(Coral-root orchids)

The name *Corallorhiza* is from the Greek words meaning "coral root," in reference to the appearance and texture of the rhizome.

A small genus of 10 to 12 species distributed mostly in North America and Central America. All are leafless, nonphotosynthetic saprophytes noted for their brilliant colors. Given the lack of leaves and variable coloration, positive identification often depends on careful observation of flower structure and dimensions. Even after the flowers have withered, adequate detail can often be restored by soaking them in hot water.

A Key to the *Corallorhiza* of Minnesota

1. Lip 2.5–4.0 mm long; lateral sepals with one nerve; petals and sepals 2.7–6.5 mm long; stem and flowers predominantly greenish yellow or brown, not brightly colored except for occasional purple spots on the lip; mature capsules 4–13 mm long; column not more than 2.5 mm long.

    2. Lip with small lateral lobes near or just below the middle; stem, ovaries, and flowers greenish (often fading in dried specimens); mature capsules 7–13 mm long; base of stems not noticeably thickened; sepals usually more than 4 mm long; occurring northward (mostly in bogs and swamps); flowering in May and June.

                                                           C. trifida

    2. Lip without lateral lobes; stem brownish, ovaries brownish or greenish; capsules 6–7 mm long; base of stem sometimes noticeably thicker than the middle; sepals usually less than 4 mm long; occurring southward (in hardwood forests); not appearing until August.

                                                        C. odontorhiza

1. Lip 4.2–13.0 mm long; lateral sepals with 3 to 5 nerves; petals and sepals 5.5–18.0 mm long; stem and/or flowers with conspicuous red or purple coloring (rarely yellow in "albino" color forms); mature capsules 11–21 mm long; column more than 2.5 mm long.

    3. Lip 4.2–7.5 mm long, with a lateral lobe on each side near the middle; petals and sepals variously colored, but not with reddish purple stripes, 5.5–10.0 mm long, 1.0–2.2 mm wide.

                                                       C. maculata

    3. Lip usually more than 7.5 mm long (range 5.5–13.0 mm), without lateral lobes; petals and sepals pale yellowish with 3 to 7 reddish purple stripes, 8–18 mm long, 1.5–6.0 mm wide.

                                                       C. striata

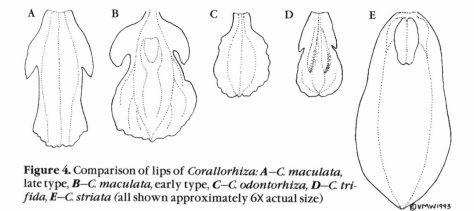

Figure 4. Comparison of lips of *Corallorhiza: A—C. maculata,* late type, *B—C. maculata,* early type, *C—C. odontorhiza, D—C. trifida, E—C. striata* (all shown approximately 6X actual size)

*Fragments of the once extensive deciduous forest
provide habitat for many orchids.*

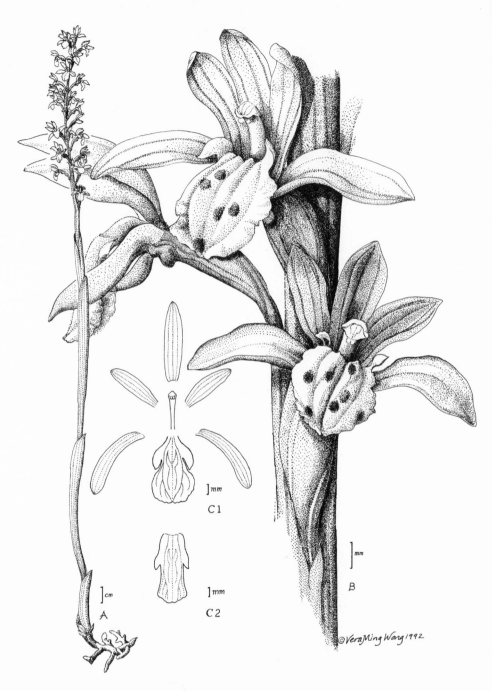

Corallorhiza maculata **A**–Flowering plant, early type, **B**–Portion of inflorescence, early type, **C1**–Flower early type, exploded view, **C2**–Lip, late type

Corallorhiza maculata (Raf.) Raf.

Common name: Spotted coral-root.

Abundance: Frequent in the northeast, occasional or rare elsewhere.

Habitat: Typically in upland coniferous or hardwood forests, but sometimes in swamp habitats; often in nutrient-poor, rocky, or shallow soils. It prefers somewhat acidic substrata, and is apparently absent or at least rare in the calcareous soils of the "Big Woods" region.

Known flowering dates: June 12-August 8.

Description: Stem 15-55 cm long (including inflorescence), reddish purple, glabrous, arising from a fragile coralloid rhizome; roots absent, functionally replaced by fine

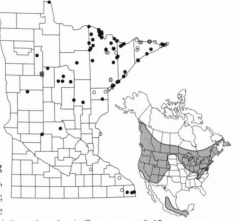

hairs on the rhizome; leaves reduced to bladeless sheaths; inflorescence 3-15 cm long, 1.5-4.0 cm wide, consisting of 6 to 51 flowers; floral bracts 0.7-3.0 mm long; ovaries 5.5-11.0 mm long, 1.0-3.0 mm wide at anthesis, pedicels 1.5-5.0 mm long, colored similar to the petals and sepals; capsule pendant, 1.1-2.0 cm long, 5.0-11.0 mm wide; sepals reddish purple, often with some greenish yellow near the base, linear to oblong or oblanceolate, three-nerved, 5.5-10.0 mm long, 1.0-2.2 mm wide; petals similar to the sepals but often paler and somewhat shorter; lip whitish, usually spotted with purple, obovate, with a prominent lateral lobe on each side below the middle, three-nerved, somewhat recurved, 4.2-7.5 mm long, 2.1-5.0 mm wide near the apex, apical margin undulate; column 2.7-6.0 mm long.

Aid to identification: In general appearance it is probably most similar to *Aplectrum hyemale*, but *Aplectrum* has a more subdued color, is generally more southern in range, and flowers earlier in the spring.

This is a variable species, and several color forms have been described: f. *flavida* (Peck) Farw., with yellow stem and flowers, and white unspotted lips; f. *intermedia* (Farw.) Farw., intermediate between f. *flavida* and the typical form; f. *punicea* (Bartlett) Weath. & Adams, with deep reddish purple stem and flowers, and pale sheaths.

There are also two distinct varieties in Minnesota (Freudenstein, 1987). One (currently unnamed) is an early flowering type with a dilated lip and longer floral bracts, longer ovaries, and longer column. It is the most common of the two, and is fairly evenly distributed across northern Minnesota (south to Pope County). The typical variety flowers, on average, two weeks later, has a proportionately narrower lip, and tends to have shorter bracts (less than 1 mm), shorter ovaries (5.5-11.0 mm), shorter column (less than 4.6 mm), and fewer flowers (less than 20). It occurs most abundantly in the northeast, but ranges south to the Iowa border.

Comments: The often brilliant colors of this orchid form a striking contrast with the typical woodland hues of green and brown, and make it a favorite with photographers. It is not difficult to find in the northeast, and is especially abundant in the state parks on the north shore of Lake Superior.

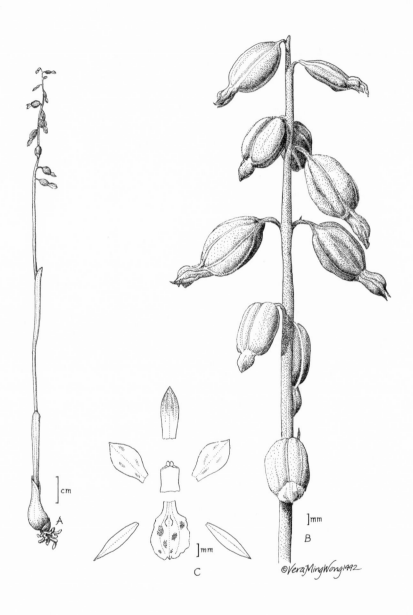

Corallorhiza odontorhiza **A**–Flowering plant, **B**–Portion of inflorescence, showing cleistogamous flowers, **C**–Cleistogamous flower, exploded view

Corallorhiza odontorhiza (Willd.) Nutt.

Common name: Autumn coral-root.

Abundance: Infrequent.

Habitat: In dry to mesic forests of the type usually dominated by oak (*Quercus*), elm (*Ulmus*), maple (*Acer*), or basswood (*Tilia*). Usually in calcareous to weakly acidic soils; in both early and late successional forests. In one example, a colony was discovered in a young forest that had been a plowed field fifteen years earlier.

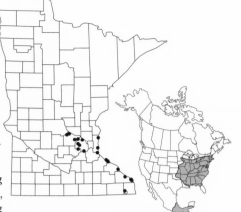

Known flowering dates: August 6-October 11.

Description: Stem 13-22 cm long (including inflorescence), brown or purplish brown, glabrous, sometimes swollen at base, arising from a fragile coralloid rhizome; roots absent; leaves reduced to bladeless sheaths; inflorescence 2-6 cm long, 1.5-2.0 cm wide, with 7-16 divergent cleistogamous flowers; floral bracts 1.5-2.0 mm long; ovaries greenish yellow to brown, 4.0-7.0 mm long, 2.5-4.5 mm wide; pedicels 1.0-3.5 mm long; capsules pendant to divergent, the same size as the ovary; sepals dark purple to greenish brown, linear-lanceolate, one-nerved, 2.7-4.5 mm long, 0.8-1.5 mm wide; petals similar to sepals but somewhat shorter and wider; lip whitish with purple markings, obovate to suborbicular, three-nerved, 2.5-3.3 mm long, 2.0-2.5 mm wide, margin entire or slightly undulate, not lobed; column 1.0-2.0 mm long.

Aid to identification: *C. odontorhiza* is often mistaken for *C. trifida.* Both are small, leafless, "nondescript" orchids with small flowers and small capsules. They differ in the color of the stem (brownish in *C. odontorhiza*, greenish in *C. trifida*), the shape of the lip (unlobed in *C. odontorhiza*, lobed in *C. trifida*), and the length of the perianth (rarely more than 4 mm long in *C. odontorhiza*, usually more than 4 mm long in *C. trifida*). Also, *C. odontorhiza* is restricted to southern upland forests and appears from early August to October, whereas *C. trifida* is more northern, is more likely to be found in bogs or swamps, and is well past flowering by July.

This remarkable plant has two distinct varieties (Freudenstein, personal communication). The more easterly variety (as yet undescribed) produces conventional chasmogamous flowers, which open to attract insect pollinators. All of the Minnesota specimens, however, belong to the typical variety, which produces only cleistogamous flowers; that is, the flowers never open. Fertilization takes place within the closed flower without the possibility of insect-aided cross-pollination (Catling, 1983a). As a result, the ovaries begin to swell and ripen immediately, and the flowers look withered from the very beginning. Orchid hunters who find this plant often think they have missed the "floral display," but there really is no display to see.

Comments: This species was first discovered in the southeastern corner of the state (Houston County) in 1899. It was not seen again until 1979, when it started turning up in several eastern and central counties. Has the plant recently expanded its range into a part of the state it had not historically occupied? Or had it been there all along but simply remained unnoticed because of its small size and late phenology?

Corallorhiza striata *A*–Flowering plant, *B*–Portion of inflorescence, *C*–Flower, exploded view

Corallorhiza striata Lindl.

Common name: Striped coral-root.

Abundance: Infrequent to occasional.

Habitat: Most often in upland forests, including a wide variety of both hardwood and coniferous types. It occurs less often in brushy thickets and swamp forests. It seems to prefer weakly acidic to circumneutral soil.

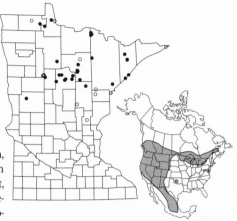

Known flowering dates: May 21-June 24.

Description: Stem 12-50 cm long (including inflorescence), reddish to brownish, glabrous, one to several arising singly from a brittle coralloid rhizome; roots absent, leaves reduced to 3 or 4 overlapping bladeless sheaths on the lower one-half or two-thirds of the stem; inflorescence a terminal raceme, 5-23 cm long, 2.2-4.2 cm wide, consisting of 7 to 26 flowers; floral bracts 1.5-6.0 mm long; ovaries 3.0-10.0 mm long, 0.7-2.5 mm wide at anthesis, on a pedicel 1.5-3.0 mm long; mature capsules pendant, 1.5-2.1 cm long, 7-9 mm wide; sepals yellowish with 3 to 7 conspicuous reddish purple stripes, linear-oblong to narrowly elliptical or somewhat obovate, 8.0-18.0 mm long, 1.5-6.0 mm wide; petals similar to the sepals; lip predominantly dark purple (actually 3 to 5 broad purplish stripes converging on a pale background), obovate to elliptical, without lateral lobes, margins entire, 5.5-13.0 mm long, 3.6-8.0 mm wide; column 3-6 mm long.

Aid to identification: This is probably the most distinctive and conspicuous of the *Corallorhizas*. The somewhat drooping petals and sepals with their characteristic red stripes on a pale background give the plant an unmistakable "candy cane" appearance. In contrast, the lip is predominantly dark purple and hangs straight down. The lip is also unique in its smooth, entire margin (which can be seen without magnification), as compared to the variously toothed, lobed, or undulating margins of the other species.

When comparing fruiting specimens, *C. striata* has measurably longer capsules (at least 1.5 cm long) than either *C. trifida* or *C. odontorhiza*, but its capsules are about the same length as those of *C. maculata*. The only hope of making a positive identification of fruiting plants may be to find a few fragments of the shriveled flower clinging to the capsule. These fragments can usually be restored to some extent by boiling in water.

In certain rare specimens the typical reddish purple color is replaced by yellowish brown (f. *fulva* Fern.).

Comments: This is the least common of the northern *Corallorhizas* but the most striking in appearance and the most sought after by photographers. Like all *Corallorhizas*, its occurrence year to year is sporadic and unpredictable. Perhaps the most reliable place to find it is along the woodland trails in Itasca State Park.

Corallorhiza trifida **A**–Flowering plant, **B**–Portion of inflorescence, **C**–Flower, exploded view

Corallorhiza trifida Chat.

Common name: Early coral-root.

Abundance: Frequent.

Habitat: It occurs most frequently in acidic to slightly calcareous bog/swamp forests, "rooted" in peat or decaying woody material. It also occurs in upland forests, both coniferous and hardwood, as well as in dry or wet thickets, forested swales, and various edge habitats.

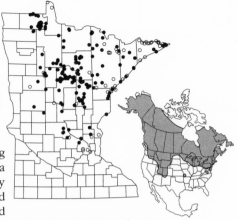

Known flowering dates: May 14-June 25.

Description: Stem 12–36 cm long (including inflorescence), greenish (often drying to a straw or chestnut color), glabrous, as many as ten arising singly from a brittle coralloid rhizome; roots absent, functionally replaced by tufts of fine hair on the rhizome; leaves reduced to 2 or 3 overlapping bladeless sheaths on the lower half of the stem; inflorescence a terminal raceme 2.5–8.0 cm long, 0.8–2.8 cm wide, consisting of 4 to 19 ascending flowers; floral bracts, 0.5–1.5 mm long; ovaries green, 3.0–7.0 mm long, 1.0–2.3 mm wide at anthesis, on short pedicels 1.0–2.5 mm long, capsules pendant, 0.7–1.4 cm long, 3–8 mm wide; sepals yellowish green, linear to oblanceolate or oblong; one-nerved, 3.2–6.5 mm long, 0.5–1.5 mm wide, the dorsal sepal somewhat wider than the lateral sepals; petals yellowish green, occasionally with purple spots, linear-oblanceolate, one- to three-nerved, 2.7–5.0 mm long, 1.1–1.6 mm wide, loosely connivent with the dorsal sepal to form a vague hood over the column; lip white, sometimes with purple spots, oblong-quadrate to obovate, with a short upturned lobe or tooth on each side near or just below the middle, three-nerved, recurved, 2.5–4.0 mm long, 1.5–2.8 mm wide, apical margin undulate; column 1.5–2.5 mm long.

Aid to identification: It is most likely to be confused with *C. odontorhiza*; both are small drab-colored plants that are more often seen in fruit than in flower. But *C. trifida* is usually well past flowering by July, and by August the ovaries are mature and shedding seeds. This is still a week or more before *C. odontorhiza* even appears above ground. *C. trifida* is also the only *Corallorhiza* that has a noticeable amount of green color (particularly on the stem, but also on the ovaries and flowers).

Paler than normal specimens with unspotted lips and narrow perianth parts have been segregated as var. *verna* (Nutt.) Fern. But according to Freudenstein (personal communication), this morphological and color variation is not consistent enough to warrant varietal status.

Comments: In spite of its small size and camouflage-like coloration, *C. trifida* is one of the most frequently encountered orchids in Minnesota. It is especially abundant in forested peatlands, where it can be found with a high degree of predictability, but it can also be found in mineral soil in a wide range of habitat types.

Like all *Corallorhizas*, *C. trifida* is an obligate saprophyte. It obtains its nutrients not from the soil, but from certain soil-inhabiting fungi that enter the plant through the hairs on the rhizome (Campbell, 1970). Unlike other *Corallorhizas* it does have some green coloring, indicating that it may perform some photosynthesis.

The Genus Cypripedium *L.*
(Lady's-slipper orchids)
❦

The name *Cypripedium* is from the Greek words meaning "Aphrodite's shoe" or "Venus's slipper," in reference to the shape of the lip.

Consisting of somewhere between thirty and fifty species; distributed widely in the Northern Hemisphere with eleven species in North America. These are among the most primitive and evolutionarily isolated of all the orchids. They are also the most popular and recognizable members of our native flora, and are easily distinguished by the trademark pouch and brightly colored flowers.

A Key to the *Cypripedium* of Minnesota

1. Leaves two per stem, basal; opening of pouch concealed in a deep longitudinal fissure on the dorsal surface.

C. acaule

1. Leaves three or more per stem, not basal; opening of pouch more or less circular, clearly visible near the base of the pouch.

   2. The two lateral sepals separate (resulting in six distinct perianth parts); the pouch 1.0-2.0 cm long (measured along the upper surface), with a conspicuous downward conical projection on the underside at the apex.

C. arietinum

   2. The two lateral sepals fused into a single sepal appearing directly below the pouch (resulting in a total of only five perianth parts); the pouch 1.7-6.0 cm long, generally obovate in shape, without a downward projection at the apex.

      3. Pouch white or pink, or some combination of both.

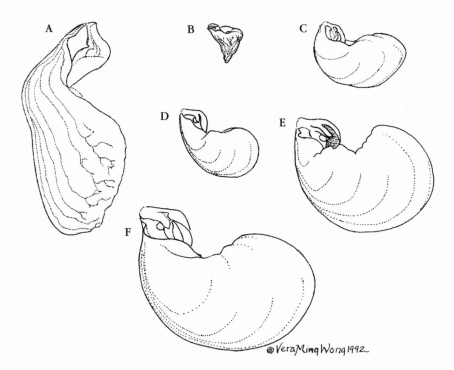

Figure 5. Floral lips (with columns) of *Cypripedium* spp.: *A—C. acaule, B—C. arietinum, C—C. candidum, D—C. calceolus* var. *parviflorum, E—C. calceolus* var. *pubescens, F—C. reginae* (all shown actual size)

4. Pouch 1.7–2.5 cm long, white; petals and sepals greenish yellow; flowering stems 10–35 cm long.

C. candidum

4. Pouch 3.0–5.5 cm long, white streaked with pink (pure white forms are known but uncommon), petals and sepals white; flowering stems 25–71 cm long.

C. reginae

3. Pouch yellow.

5. Pouch 1.6–3.0 cm long; dorsal sepal 2.0–4.0 cm long; lateral sepal 1.9–3.6 cm long; petals 2.5–5.0 cm long; petals and sepals reddish brown (the color of dried blood), usually with yellowish green streaks.

C. calceolus var. *parviflorum*

5. Pouch 2.2–6.0 cm long; dorsal sepal 3.5–7.0 cm long; lateral sepal 3.2–6.5 cm long; petals 4.5–9.5 cm long; petals and sepals mostly yellowish green with reddish brown streaks.

C. calceolus var. *pubescens*

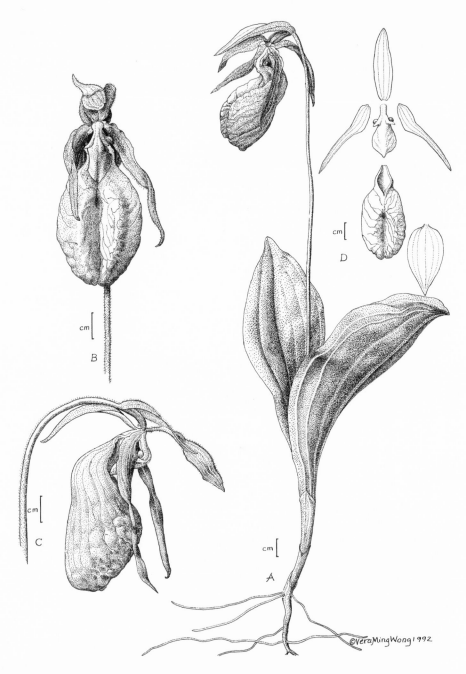

Cypripedium acaule **A**–Flowering plant, **B**–Flower, front view, **C**–Flower, side view, **D**–Flower, exploded view

Cypripedium acaule Ait.

Common name: Stemless lady's-slipper.

Abundance: Relatively common.

Habitat: Ubiquitous in a wide variety of northern forest habitats, from dry sandy pine forests to the wettest coniferous bogs/swamps. The only obvious requirements are shade and an acidic, nutrient-poor substrate.

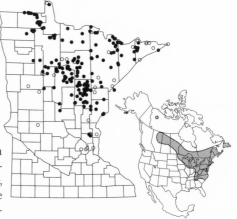

Known flowering dates: May 24-July 10.

Description: Stem (peduncle) 14-44 cm long, glandular-pubescent; arising from a coarse, knotty rhizome; roots long and cord-like; leaves two, basal, elliptical to obovate, 9-23 cm long, 2.5-9.0 cm wide; inflorescence a single nodding flower; floral bract lanceo-late, green, 2.3-4.5 cm long, 3.5-11.0 mm wide near the base; ovary 1.0-1.5 cm long, 4.0-6.0 mm wide at anthesis; sepals elliptical to lance-elliptical, yellowish green to brown or purple, 2.5-4.0 cm long, 0.9-1.6 cm wide, the two lateral sepals fused to form a single sepal located ventrally (directly below the lip); petals lanceolate to lance-linear, acuminate, similar in color to the sepals, 2.8-4.5 cm long, 5.0-9.0 mm wide; lip an inflated pouch, pink to purple, obovate, 3.3-6.0 cm long, the opening concealed in a deep longitudinal fissure on the dorsal surface.

Aid to identification: This is the only lady's-slipper with two basal leaves; the others have three or more alternate leaves that are scattered over most of the stem. The deep longitudinal crease on the top of the pouch is also unique to this species.

The term "stemless," as used in the common name, is confusing to many people. What may appear to be a stem is actually a peduncle or scape. The true stem is a short underground structure that is usually not visible.

In the normal developmental process, the unexpanded pouch of all young flowers of *C. acaule* first appears white, but becomes pink with maturity (Baldwin, 1970). A true albino form does exist in which the pouch remains pure white, and the petals and sepals are yellowish green. This form (f. *albiflora* Rand & Redfield) is quite rare in Minnesota (Lakela, 1951), but could be found singly or as scattered individuals in any colony of normal-colored plants.

Comments: This is one of the most common orchids in Minnesota, and certainly is the most frequently seen lady's-slipper. It is also one of the few orchids for which we have any life-history information. According to Curtis (1943), the seeds may remain dormant for several years before conditions are favorable for germination. Following germination the young plant (corm) undergoes a remarkable developmental period entirely underground, nourished by a symbiotic (possibly parasitic) relationship with a specialized fungus. During the third or fourth year after germination the plant may send up its first green leaf, and sometime after the eighth year it will produce its first flower. It is not known how long individuals can live, but it is likely that they can survive for decades if their habitat is not disturbed.

C. acaule is known to be pollinated by bumblebees (Stoutamire, 1967).

Cypripedium arientinum **A**–Flowering plant, **B**–Flower, **C**–Flower, exploded view

Cypripedium arietinum R. Br.

Common name: Ram's-head lady's-slipper.

Abundance: Rare. Listed as endangered in Minnesota. Report all sightings to the Minnesota DNR.

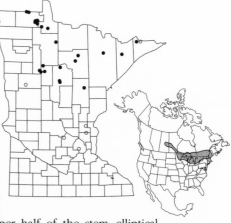

Habitat: Occurring in a wide range of forest types, including dry sandy jack pine forests, coniferous/*Sphagnum* swamps, spruce-fir forests, and mixed conifer-hardwood uplands. There are also records from thin-soil barrens on ice-scoured granite bedrock in the northeast.

Known flowering dates: May 20-June 26.

Description: Stems 15-32 cm long, pubescent, up to 12 arising from a single coarse, knotty rhizome; roots numerous, long and cordlike; leaves 3 to 5, mostly on the upper half of the stem, elliptical, 5.0-10.0 cm long, 1.4-3.0 cm wide; inflorescence of one or occasionally two flowers; floral bract green, foliaceous, elliptical to lance-ovate, 2.9-6.0 cm long, 0.7-1.6 cm wide; ovary 1.0-1.7 cm long, 2.0-4.0 mm wide at anthesis; dorsal sepal greenish to purplish, ovate to lance-ovate, acute, 1.2-2.6 cm long, 5.0-13.0 mm wide; lateral sepals separate, greenish to purplish, lance-acuminate, 1.2-2.1 cm long, 1.8-3.0 mm wide; petals similar to the lateral sepals; lip an inflated pouch, whitish or pinkish with prominent purple veins, with a conspicuous downward conical projection on the underside at the apex, 1.0-2.0 cm long, the opening of the pouch surrounded by white silky hairs.

Aid to identification: This is the smallest and rarest of our lady's-slippers, and also the most distinctive. Once seen it will not easily be mistaken for any other species. The most notable feature is the shape of the minute lip or "pouch," which, with a little imagination, looks like the head of a charging ram. This unique shape is the result of a peculiar downward projection near the end of the pouch, the exact function of which is unknown. The singular nature of the pouch is enhanced by the network of purple veins on a whitish background, and by the white silky hairs around the opening. This is also the only Minnesota lady's-slipper without fused lateral sepals. As a result, there are six distinct perianth parts: the lip, two petals, and three sepals. The other species have a lip, two petals, and two sepals.

Comments: Even though it occurs in a large number of habitat types, *C. arietinum* is a very rare plant. Furthermore, with its small size and camouflage coloration it is surprisingly difficult to see, even when standing directly over it. This all contributes to its mythical reputation, which makes it one of the most sought after orchids in Minnesota. Despite this intense interest, this plant has not been found south of Aitkin County since 1933, giving rise to speculation that it may now be extinct in the southern half of Minnesota.

C. arietinum is reported to be pollinated by small bees of the genus *Dialictus* (Stoutamire, 1967).

Cypripedium calceolus var. *parviflorum* **A**–Flowering plant, **B**–Flower, **C**–
Flower, exploded view

Cypripedium calceolus L. var. *parviflorum* (Salisb.) Fern.

Synonym: *Cypripedium parviflorum* Salisb.

Common name: Small yellow lady's-slipper.

Abundance: Occasional to locally frequent.

Habitat: Coniferous/*Sphagnum* swamps, meadows, fens, moist prairies, and occasionally upland coniferous or hardwood forests. It occurs in both shade and direct sunlight, in peat and mineral soil.

Known flowering dates: May 18-June 30.

Description: Stems 12-43 cm long, glandular-pubescent, up to 10 or more arising from a horizontal rhizome; roots numerous, long and cordlike; leaves 2 to 5 per stem, ovate to

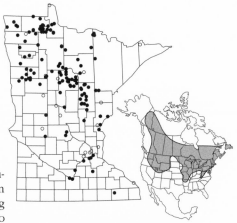

elliptical, 6.0-16.0 cm long, 2.5-8.0 cm wide; inflorescence of one or rarely two flowers; floral bract green, foliaceous, ovate to ovate-elliptical, 2.5-7.0 cm long, 0.6-2.5 cm wide; ovary 1.3-2.5 cm long, 1.5-4.0 mm wide at anthesis; dorsal sepal ovate, acuminate, dark red or reddish brown, often with streaks of yellowish green, 2.0-4.0 cm long, 0.5-1.7 cm wide; lateral sepals fused to form a single sepal located ventrally (directly below the lip), shallowly notched at the tip, otherwise similar to the dorsal sepal but somewhat smaller; petals lance-linear, often spirally twisted, the same color as the sepals, 2.5-5.0 cm long, 3.0-6.0 cm wide; lip an inflated pouch, yellow, obovate, 1.6-3.0 cm long.

Aid to identification: This is essentially a smaller version of the more familiar *C. calceolus* var. *pubescens*, but with sepals and petals dark red instead of yellowish green.

Comments: The two extreme versions of *C. calceolus* are sometimes considered to represent distinct species, or more often are considered varieties of the typical European plant (as is done here). There is even biological justification for lumping them into a single polymorphic taxon. Regardless of how botanists classify them, any absolute distinction is probably illusory. This becomes apparent when the two occur in mixed populations and the full range of intermediate sizes and colors is seen. This is probably a result of hybridization and backcrosses between the two varieties and their progeny, or it may be the result of a genetic relationship not yet understood.

   C. calceolus var. *parviflorum* also hybridizes with *C. candidum* to produce an offspring (*C. X andrewsii* Fuller) with a more or less white pouch and intermediate-colored petals and sepals (Klier et al., 1991).

   According to Curtis (1943), individuals may flower as soon as nine years after germination, but twelve years may be average.

   The glandular hairs on the stem and leaves of both varieties of *C. calceolus* are said to produce a rash upon contact with a susceptible person (MacDougal, 1895).

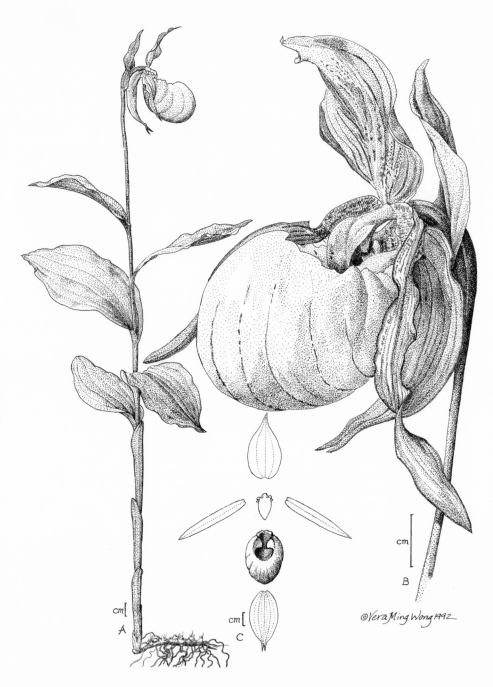

Cypripedium calceolus var. *pubescens* **A**—Flowering plant, **B**—Flower, **C**—Flower, exploded view

Cypripedium calceolus L. var. *pubescens* (Willd.) Correll

Synonym: *Cypripedium parviflorum* Salisb. var. *pubescens* (Willd.) Knight; *Cypripedium pubescens* Willd.

Common name: Large yellow lady's-slipper.

Abundance: Relatively common.

Habitat: Perhaps most common in mesic hardwood forests, but also in coniferous/*Sphagnum* swamps, hardwood swamps, meadows, prairies, and thickets.

Known flowering dates: May 10-July 12.

Description: Stems 18-60 cm long, glandular-pubescent, one to several arising from a horizontal rhizome; roots numerous, long and cordlike; leaves 3 to 6 per stem, ovate to elliptical, 8.0-20.0 cm long, 3.5-10.0 cm wide;

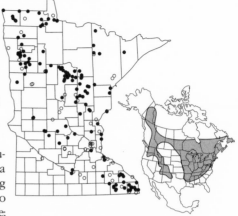

inflorescence of one or rarely two flowers; floral bract green, foliaceous, ovate to ovate-elliptical, 4.0-10.0 cm long, 0.7-4.0 cm wide; ovary 2.0-3.5 cm long, 4.0-5.0 mm wide at anthesis; dorsal sepal ovate, acuminate, yellowish green, usually with reddish brown streaks; 3.5-7.0 cm long, 1.0-3.0 cm wide; lateral sepals fused to form a single sepal located ventrally (directly below the lip), shallowly notched at the tip, otherwise similar to the dorsal sepal; petals lance-linear, often spirally twisted, the same color as the sepals, 4.5-9.5 cm long, 4.0-10.0 mm wide; lip an inflated pouch, yellow, obovate, 2.2-6.0 cm long.

Aid to identification: This and *C. calceolus* var. *parviflorum* are the only yellow-flowered lady's-slippers in Minnesota and can only be confused with each other. The size of the pouch is important, but not conclusive, in distinguishing the two varieties. If the pouch is large (over 3 cm long), it is almost certainly var. *pubescens*, but if the pouch is small (under 3 cm long), it may be var. *parviflorum* or simply a small specimen of var. *pubescens*. The petals and sepals of var. *parviflorum* are also generally smaller and of a more uniform dark color, but these characters are not always corollated.

Comments: In the southern part of the state var. *pubescens* generally occurs in upland forests, and var. *parviflorum* usually in open wetlands (fens, seeps, meadows, and so on). In the north, especially the northwest, the two varieties often grow side by side in the same habitat. In this situation plants are often found with intermediate tepal color and pouch size. This confusing situation is frequently blamed on hybridization between the two varieties, or sometimes as the expression of the normal variability within a single polymorphic taxon.

C. calceolus var. *pubescens* also hybridizes with *C. candidum*, producing offspring with intermediate characters. This hybrid is sometimes referred to as *C. Xflavillianum* Curtis, but a more acceptable name may be *C. Xandrewsii* Fuller (Voss, 1966).

Var. *pubescens* is reported to be pollinated by a variety of small bees (Stoutamire, 1967), presumably in the same way as var. *parviflorum*. The degree of pollinator isolation is unknown, but var. *parviflorum* appears to flower about one week earlier than var. *pubescens*.

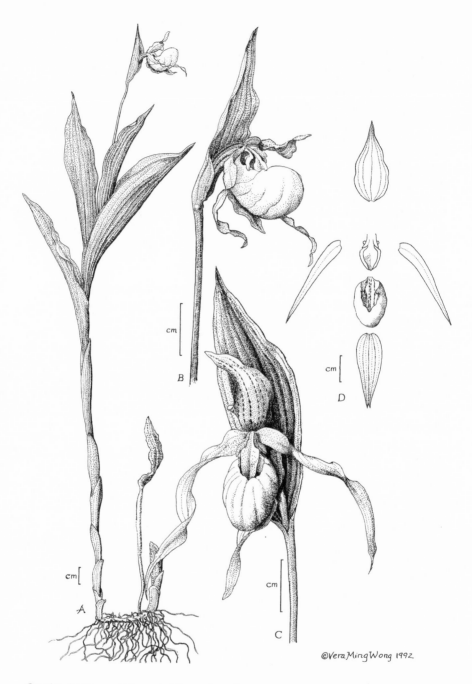

Cypripedium candidum **A**–Flowering plant, **B**–Flower, **C**–Flower, front view, **D**–Flower, exploded view

Cypripedium candidum Muhl. ex Willd.

Common name: Small white lady's-slipper.

Abundance: Declining. Restricted to small remnants of original habitat.

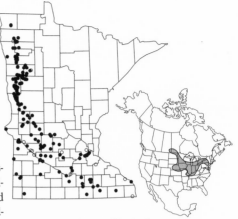

Habitat: This is primarily a species of moist prairies, but within the prairie region it also occurs in sedge meadows and calcareous fens. There are a few anomalous records from the Paleozoic Plateau in the southeast, where it occurs in dry gravelly bluff prairies.

Known flowering dates: May 19-June 22.

Description: Stems 10-35 cm long, pubescent, up to 50 or more arising from a horizontal rhizome; roots numerous, long and cordlike; leaves 2 to 4 per stem, with an additional 2 to 4 bladeless sheaths below, narrowly ovate to lance-elliptical or elliptical, 5.0-15.0 cm long, 2.0-6.0 cm wide, inflorescence of one or rarely two flowers; floral bract green, foliaceous, narrowly elliptical, 3.3-11.0 cm long, 0.9-3.2 cm wide; ovary 1.4-2.3 cm long, 2.5-3.0 mm wide at anthesis; dorsal sepal ovate to elliptical, greenish yellow, 1.7-2.5 cm long, 0.5-1.4 cm wide; lateral sepals fused to form a single sepal located ventrally (directly below the lip), the tip split, otherwise similar to the dorsal sepal; petals lance-linear, similar in color to the sepals, 2.1-4.1 cm long, 2.4-4.0 mm wide; lip an inflated pouch, white, occasionally with faint purple veins or spots, obovate, 1.7-2.5 cm long.

Aid to identification: The pouch will sometimes have a few faint purple markings showing through from the inside, but otherwise it is a pure glossy white, which distinguishes it from all other Minnesota lady's-slippers. The pouch is also quite small (not more than 2.5 cm long), much smaller than one would expect from seeing it only in photographs.

Putative hybrids with *C. calceolus* var. *pubescens* and *C. calceolus* var. *parviflorum* (*C.* X*andrewsii* Fuller) are not uncommon, especially in the northwestern counties where all three taxa may grow side by side. These hybrids all have more or less white pouches, but the petals and sepals are intermediate in color between the respective parents.

Comments: This species has become quite rare throughout most of its range. Only in Minnesota is it still possible to stand in a prairie and see tens of thousands of small white lady's-slippers in a single view. Yet, this seeming abundance represents less than 1 percent of the original. The rest was plowed under for the benefit of agriculture, a practice that is continuing unabated.

Like most lady's-slippers, *C. candidum* is a very slow growing, long-lived plant that requires an estimated twelve years or more to reach maturity (Curtis, 1943). The age of some of the larger plants, those with fifty or more stems, can only be guessed.

It is reported to be pollinated by small andrenid and halictine bees (Catling and Knerer, 1980).

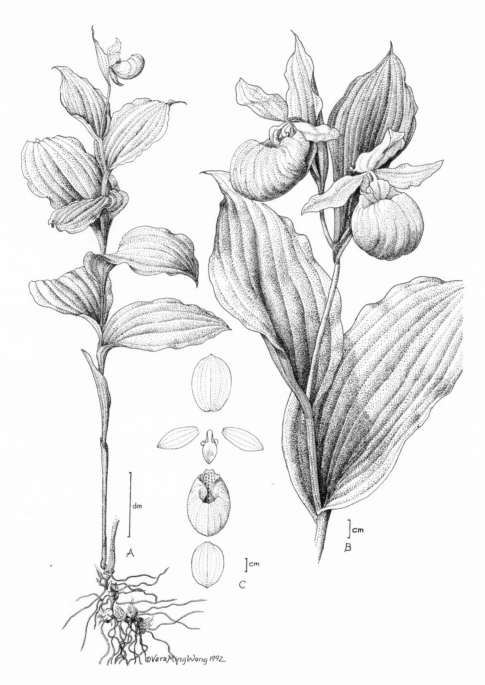

Cypripedium reginae **A**–Flowering plant, **B**–Double flowered plant, **C**–Flower, exploded view

Cypripedium reginae Walt.

Common name: Showy lady's-slipper.

Abundance: Occasional to locally frequent.

Habitat: Typically in coniferous swamps, hardwood swamps, seeps, sedge meadows, fens, shrub swamps, and floating mats. It is also an effective colonizer of moist habitats in roadside ditches. It seems to require weakly acidic to weakly calcareous soil (either organic or mineral), and occurs in both shade and direct sunlight.

Known flowering dates: June 7-July 11.

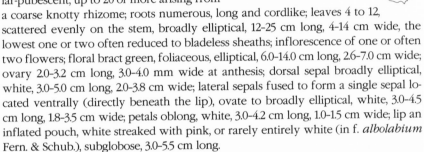

Description: Stems 25-71 cm long, glandular-pubescent, up to 20 or more arising from a coarse knotty rhizome; roots numerous, long and cordlike; leaves 4 to 12, scattered evenly on the stem, broadly elliptical, 12-25 cm long, 4-14 cm wide, the lowest one or two often reduced to bladeless sheaths; inflorescence of one or often two flowers; floral bract green, foliaceous, elliptical, 6.0-14.0 cm long, 2.6-7.0 cm wide; ovary 2.0-3.2 cm long, 3.0-4.0 mm wide at anthesis; dorsal sepal broadly elliptical, white, 3.0-5.0 cm long, 2.0-3.8 cm wide; lateral sepals fused to form a single sepal located ventrally (directly beneath the lip), ovate to broadly elliptical, white, 3.0-4.5 cm long, 1.8-3.5 cm wide; petals oblong, white, 3.0-4.2 cm long, 1.0-1.5 cm wide; lip an inflated pouch, white streaked with pink, or rarely entirely white (in f. *albolabium* Fern. & Schub.), subglobose, 3.0-5.5 cm long.

Aid to identification: This is Minnesota's state flower, and its likeness is certainly familiar to everyone in the state. It has been seen on the official state flag, the state seal, a U.S. postage stamp, and a variety of other government emblems. It is also the logo for countless commercial enterprises and social organizations, not to mention its appearance on T-shirts, coffee mugs, bath towels, and so on.

It is easily distinguished by its large overall size and by the color of its flower. The pure white petals and sepals are unique among Minnesota lady's-slippers, as is the combination of pink and white on the pouch.

Comments: The popularity of the showy lady's-slipper has led to its decline via the illicit orchid trade. Unsuspecting gardeners buy "nursery-propagated" orchids, not realizing that the plants were actually taken from the wild. Only plants raised from tissue cultures offer a nondestructive alternative to wild collecting (Brumback, 1990).

In its natural habitat an individual requires at least 14 to 16 years to produce its first flower (Curtis, 1943). If left undisturbed the rhizome will continue to grow and produce more stems in successive years. As a result, the large "clumps" of 20 or more stems that are often seen in cedar swamps may be as much as a hundred years old, possibly much older.

. The soft glandular hairs of the leaves are capable of producing a poison-ivy-like rash in susceptible persons (MacDougal, 1895).

It is reported to be pollinated by bees (Stoutamire, 1967).

Amerorchis rotundifolia, small round-leaved orchis (photo by R. Haug)

Aplectrum hyemale,
putty root (photo by
R. Haug)

Aplectrum hyemale, putty root, leaves (photo by R. Haug)

Arethusa bulbosa, dragon's-mouth
(photo by R. Haug)

Calopogon tuberosus, grass-pink
(photo by R. Haug)

Calypso bulbosa var. *americana,* fairy slipper (photo by J. Pennoyer)

Coeloglossum viride
var. ***virescens,*** long-bracted orchid (photo by
D. Plunkett)

Coeloglossum viride var. ***virescens,***
long-bracted orchid (photo by
D. Plunkett)

Corallorhiza maculata, spotted coral-root (photo by R. Haug)

Corallorhiza odontorhiza, autumn coral-root (photo by R. Haug)

Corallorhiza striata, striped coral-
root (photo by J. Mathisen)

Corallorhiza trifida, early coral-root
(photo by D. Plunkett)

Cypripedium acaule, stemless lady's-slipper (photo by R. Haug)

Cypripedium arietinum, ram's-head lady's-slipper (photo by R. Haug)

Cypripedium calceolus var. *parviflorum,* small yellow lady's-slipper (photo by W. Smith)

Cypripedium calceolus var. *pubescens,* large yellow lady's-slipper (photo by J. Mathisen)

Cypripedium candidum, small white lady's-slipper (photo by R. Haug)

Cypripedium reginae,
showy lady's-slipper
(photo by R. Haug)

Galearis spectabilis, showy orchis (photo by W. Smith)

Goodyera pubescens, downy rattlesnake plantain (photo by W. Smith)

Goodyera pubescens, rosette, downy rattlesnake plantain (photo by W. Smith)

Goodyera repens var. *ophioides,* lesser rattlesnake plantain (photo by W. Smith)

Goodyera repens var. *ophioides,* rosette, lesser rattlesnake plantain (photo by R. Haug)

Goodyera tesselata, tesselated rattlesnake plantain (photo by R. Haug)

Goodyera tesselata, rosette, tesselated rattlesnake plantain
(photo by W. Smith)

Liparis lilifolia, lily-leaved twayblade (photo by W. Smith)

Liparis loeselii, Loesel's twayblade
(photo by W. Smith)

Listera auriculata, auricled twayblade (photo by W. Smith)

Listera convallarioides,
broad-leaved twayblade
(photo by W. Smith)

Listera convallarioides, broad-leaved
twayblade (photo by W. Smith)

Listera cordata, heart-leaved twayblade
(photo by W. Smith)

Malaxis monophyllos var.
brachypoda, white adder's-
mouth (photo by W. Smith)

Malaxis paludosa, bog adder's-mouth (photo by W. Smith)

Malaxis paludosa, bog adder's-mouth (photo by W. Smith)

Malaxis unifolia, green adder's-mouth (photo by R. Haug)

Platanthera clavellata, small green wood-orchid (photo by R. Haug)

Platanthera dilatata, tall white bog-orchid (photo by W. Smith)

Platanthera flava var. ***herbiola,***
tubercled rein-orchid (photo by
W. Smith)

Platanthera hookeri, Hooker's
orchid (photo by W. Smith)

Platanthera hyperborea,
northern bog-orchid (photo by
R. Haug)

Platanthera hyperborea, northern
bog-orchid (photo by R. Haug)

Platanthera lacera, ragged fringed-orchid (photo by R. Haug)

Platanthera obtusata, small
northern bog-orchid (photo by
W. Smith)

Platanthera obtusata, small northern
bog-orchid (photo by W. Smith)

Platanthera orbiculata,
large round-leaved orchid
(photo by W. Smith)

Platanthera orbiculata, large round-
leaved orchid (photo by W. Smith)

Platanthera praeclara, western prairie fringed-orchid (photo by W. Smith)

Platanthera psycodes, small purple
fringed-orchid (photo by R. Haug)

Platanthera psycodes, white
form, small purple fringed-orchid
(photo by D. Plunkett)

Pogonia ophioglossoides, rose pogonia (photo by R. Haug)

Spiranthes cernua, nodding
ladies'-tresses (photo by W. Smith)

Spiranthes lacera, northern
slender ladies'-tresses
(photo by J. Mathisen)

Spiranthes magnicamporum, Great Plains ladies'-tresses (photo by W. Smith)

Spiranthes romanzoffiana, hooded ladies'-tresses (photo by W. Smith)

The Genus Galearis *Raf.*
❦

The name *Galearis* is from the Latin word meaning helmet, in reference to the hood formed by the connivent sepals and petals.

Historically placed in the large and inclusive genus *Orchis,* but subsequently segregated because of morphological differences in the column and the absence of tuberoids. As currently defined, the genus *Galearis* comprises only two species: one in North America, the other in eastern Asia.

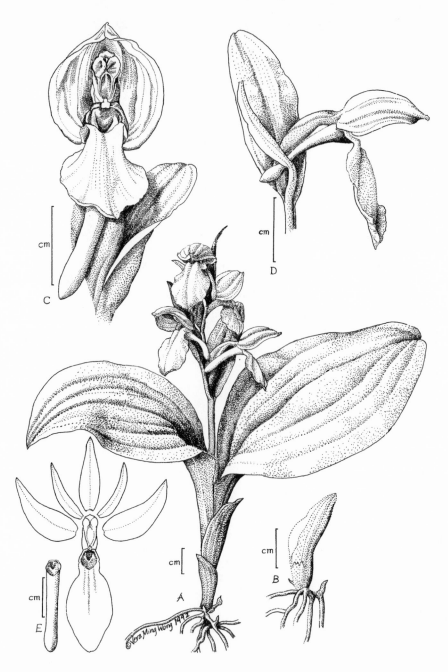

Galearis spectabilis **A**–Flowering plant, **B**–Stem and root, with new shoot on rhizome, **C**–Flower, front view (from below), **D**–Flower, side view, **E**–Flower, exploded view

Galearis spectabilis (L.) Raf.

Synonym: *Orchis spectabilis* L.

Common name: Showy orchis.

Abundance: Occasional to frequent.

Habitat: Found almost exclusively in mesic hardwood forests; typically under a closed canopy of oak (*Quercus*), maple (*Acer*), elm (*Ulmus*), ash (*Fraxinus*), or basswood (*Tilia*). It prefers loamy soil that is well drained and weakly acidic or calcareous.

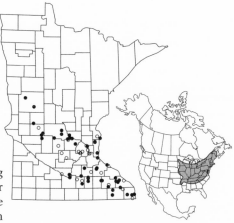

Known flowering dates: May 11-June 10.

Description: Stem 8-25 cm long (including inflorescence), glabrous; leaves two per stem, somewhat succulent, basal, obovate to elliptical or nearly orbicular, 8-20 cm long, 2-9 cm wide; inflorescence a terminal raceme, 4-8 cm long, 3.5-5.5 cm wide, consisting of 2 to 10 purple and white flowers; floral bracts leaflike, lanceolate to elliptical, 2.5-6.5 cm long, 0.8-2.0 cm wide; ovaries 1.2-2.0 cm long; sepals purple, elliptical to ovate, 1.2-1.9 cm long, 5.0-6.5 mm wide, connivent with the petals to form an arching hood; petals purple, linear, 1.0-1.8 cm long, 2.5-4.0 mm wide; lip white, ovate to orbicular, constricted near base, 1.1-2.0 cm long, 6.5-12.0 mm wide, producing a club-shaped (clavate) spur 1.2-1.8 cm long.

Aid to identification: This is one of our most distinctive and recognizable orchids and should not be confused with any other species. *Liparis lilifolia* is superficially similar in having two somewhat succulent basal leaves, and flowers with a relatively broad lip (white in *G. spectabilis* and purple in *L. lilifolia*). In *G. spectabilis*, however, the petals and sepals are united to form a hood, and the lip has an obvious spur at the base. In *L. lilifolia* the petals and sepals are free and wide-spreading, and the lip does not have a spur. The petals and sepals of *G. spectabilis* are typically purple, but pure white specimens are occasionally found, as are plants with intermediate color.

Comments: This is one of the first orchids to flower each year, often reaching anthesis before the trees have fully leafed out. It is also one of the few orchids that can still be found easily in the woodlots and parks around the Twin Cities metropolitan area. In ideal habitat it may form dense colonies of 5 to 10 tightly packed individuals with several colonies occurring on a single hillside.

It is known to be pollinated by bumblebees (Van Der Pijl and Dodson, 1966), but it is probably pollinated by other nonspecialized nectar-feeding insects as well.

The Genus Goodyera *R. Br.* *(Rattlesnake plantain orchids)*

The name *Goodyera* is in honor of John Goodyer (1592-1664), an English botanist.

About 25 species worldwide. Four species occur in North America, of which three are known to occur in Minnesota. The fourth species, *G. oblongifolia* Raf., has been reported to occur in Minnesota (Luer, 1975), but without supporting evidence. It is known to occur in Wisconsin and Ontario, and it is possible that undiscovered populations may exist in northeastern Minnesota. It is most similar in appearance to *G. tesselata* Lodd., but instead of the familiar white reticulate pattern on the leaf it has only a white band along the midrib.

A Key to the *Goodyera* of Minnesota

1. Inflorescence essentially one-sided (secund), that is, all the flowers pointed in the same direction or at least within a single 180° arc perpendicular to the axis of the stem (a character sometimes obscured in pressed specimens), or occasionally arranged in a spiral with one or fewer twists.

2. Flowering stem (including inflorescence) not more than 19 cm long; inflorescence 3–7 cm long, with fewer than 25 flowers; leaves usually 3.0 cm long or less (range 1.5–3.6 cm); floral lip globe-shaped, essentially spherical (exclusive of beak).

G. repens var. *ophioides*

2. Flowering stem usually more than 19 cm long; inflorescence 5–17 cm long, often with 25 or more flowers; the largest leaves on each plant more than 3.0 cm long (including petioles); lip more elongate, longer than wide.

G. tesselata

1. Inflorescence not distinctly one-sided or spiraled, the flowers radiating equally in all directions perpendicular to the stem.

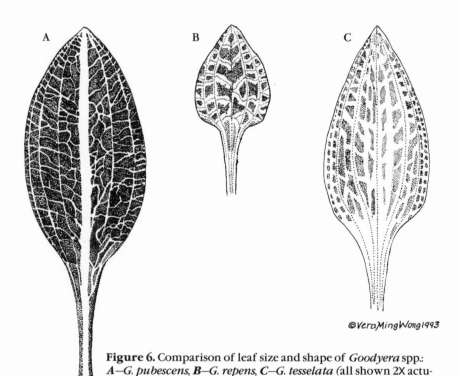

©VeraMingWong1993

Figure 6. Comparison of leaf size and shape of *Goodyera* spp.: A—*G. pubescens*, B—*G. repens*, C—*G. tesselata* (all shown 2X actual size)

3. The lowest 5 cm of the inflorescence typically with 15 or more flowers; stem (including inflorescence) often more than 30 cm long (range 24–40 cm); leaves bright green, the larger ones usually 2.0 cm wide or more; lip globe-shaped, essentially spherical (excluding beak); occurring in deciduous forests (rarely pine) in southern and central Minnesota, generally absent from northern boreal-type habitats.

G. pubescens

3. The lowest 5 cm of the inflorescence typically with 15 or fewer flowers; stem usually less than 30 cm long (range 18–32 cm); leaves bluish green, usually 2.0 cm wide or less; lip more elongated, longer than wide or high; occurring in boreal-type coniferous forests in the northern one-third of the state.

G. tesselata

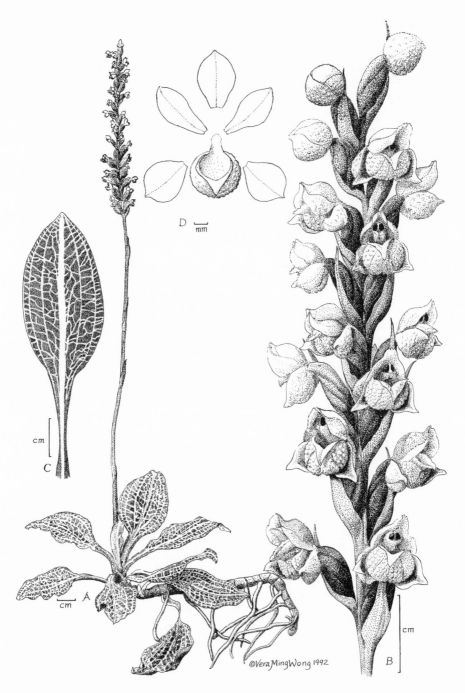

Goodyera pubescens **A**–Flowering plant, **B**–Inflorescence, **C**–Leaf, **D**–Flower, exploded view

Goodyera pubescens (Willd.) R. Br.

Common name: Downy rattlesnake plantain.

Abundance: Occasional.

Habitat: Typically in dry to mesic hardwood forests. Usually favoring the acidic soils of oak-aspen-birch forests rather than the calcareous soils of the maple-basswood "Big Woods." It is also found in native pine stands, and rarely in pine plantations.

Known flowering dates: July 30-September 1.

Description: Stems 24-40 cm long (including inflorescence), densely pubescent, arising singly from a branching horizontal rhizome; leaves 3 to 10 per stem, elliptical to

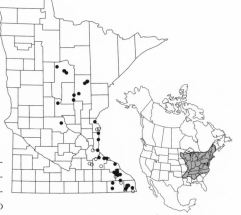

ovate or lance-ovate, 3.5-9.2 cm long, 1.3-3.0 cm wide, bright green with white reticulation along the veins, essentially basal, forming an evergreen rosette that withers after producing a flowering stem; inflorescence a dense spicate raceme, cylindrical, 5.5-12.5 cm long, 1.5-2.0 cm wide, consisting of 28 to 52 white flowers; ovaries 5.5-8.0 mm long, 1.5-3.0 mm wide at anthesis (becoming nearly globose when mature); sepals ovate to oblong-elliptical, 4.0-5.5 mm long, 3.0-4.0 mm wide; petals oblong-spatulate, 5.0-6.0 mm long, 2.5-3.5 mm wide, connivent with the dorsal sepal to form a hood over the lip; lip globular-saccate, contracted at the apex to form a short beak 0.1-0.7 mm long, entire lip 3.3-4.5 mm long, 3.0-3.5 mm wide.

Aid to identification: Similar to the other *Goodyera*s, especially *G. tesselata*, but *G. pubescens* is a taller plant with larger and proportionately broader and more rounded leaves. Also, the reticulate pattern on the leaves of *G. pubescens* is more pronounced, with the white tissue along the veins appearing in sharp contrast to the deep green background. The reticulate pattern in *G. tesselata* is less pronounced, often not even noticeable in dried specimens.

The shape of the lip (globular in *G. pubescens* and somewhat more elongated in *G. tesselata*) is probably the most reliable character, but it is prone to misinterpretation and is useful to the beginner only if known specimens are available for comparison. A more practical character is the number of flowers on the lower 5 cm of the inflorescence: *G. pubescens* usually has 15 or more, and *G. tesselata* has 15 or fewer.

Comments: The geographic ranges of *G. pubescens* and *G. tesselata* do not generally overlap in Minnesota, except in the vicinity of Aitkin and Cass counties. In that area, it is possible that hybrids may occur, but none has yet been found.

Goodyera repens var. ***ophioides*** *A*—Flowering plant, with rhizomes and sterile shoot, *B*—Portion of inflorescence, *C*—Leaf, *D*—Flower, sagittal section, *E*—Flower, exploded view

Goodyera repens (L.) R. Br. var. *ophioides* Fern.

Common name: Lesser rattlesnake plantain.

Abundance: Occasional to frequent.

Habitat: Most commonly in coniferous swamps and bogs, but also in dry to mesic upland forests, of either coniferous or mixed coniferous-hardwood types. There are also records from mossy cliffs and rock ledges. The essential requirements appear to be a cool, nutrient-poor, acidic substrate and full to partial shade.

Known flowering dates: July 14-September 9.

Description: Stems 8.0–19.0 cm long (including inflorescence), pubescent, arising singly from a branching horizontal rhizome;

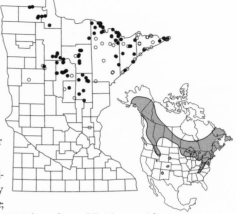

leaves 3 to 8 per stem, ovate to lance-ovate, 1.5–3.6 cm long, 0.7–1.5 cm wide, dark green with white or pale green reticulation along the veins, essentially basal, forming an evergreen rosette; inflorescence a dense to loose spicate raceme, 3.0–7.0 cm long, 0.6–1.2 cm wide, secund, consisting of up to 25 white flowers; ovaries 4.5–7.0 mm long, 2.0–2.5 mm wide at anthesis; sepals ovate to oblong or elliptical, 3.0–3.5 mm long, 1.0–2.5 mm wide; petals oblong-spatulate, 3.0–3.5 mm long, 1.0–1.5 mm wide, connivent with the dorsal sepal to form a hood over the lip; lip deeply saccate, contracted above the middle to form a beak up to 2 mm long, entire lip 2.7–3.5 mm long, about 2 mm wide.

Aid to identification: Most likely to be mistaken for *G. tesselata*, but typical or "pure" specimens of *G. repens* var. *ophioides* are rather easy to distinguish by the shorter stem, shorter inflorescence, and smaller leaves (see dichotomy 2 of the *Goodyera* key). The flowers of *G. repens* var. *ophioides* also tend to be smaller and fewer in number, and the inflorescence is usually more strongly one-sided.

Apparent hybrids and backcrosses between *G. repens* var. *ophioides* and *G. tesselata* are relatively common, resulting in specimens that are intermediate in appearance. Such hybrids can be very frustrating and even impossible to key out with confidence.

Our plants, as described here, are variety *ophioides* Fern., which differs from the typical variety in having leaves with the familiar white-on-green reticulate pattern.

Comments: The impressive record of hybridization within the genus *Goodyera* can probably be credited to the bumblebee, the most likely pollinator of all our species (Kallunki, 1981).

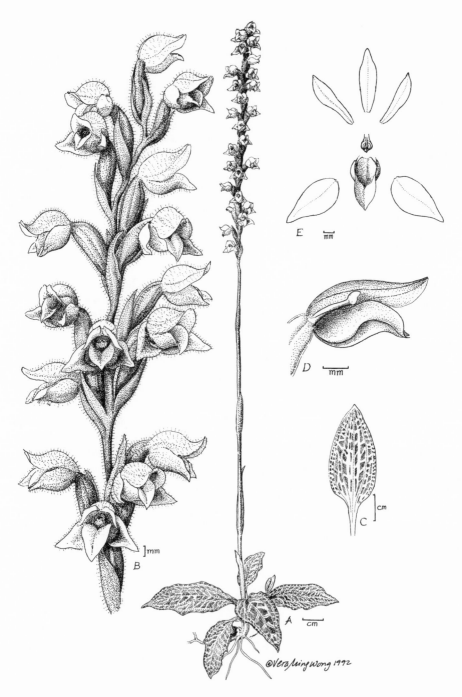

Goodyera tesselata *A*–Flowering plant, *B*–Inflorescence, *C*–Leaf, *D*–Flower, longitudinal section, *E*–Flower, exploded view

Goodyera tesselata Lodd.

Common name: Tesselated rattlesnake plantain.

Abundance: Occasional to frequent.

Habitat: Typical of jack pine (*Pinus banksiana*) forests, usually in dry sandy soil, but also in red pine (*Pinus resinosa*), white pine (*Pinus strobus*), mixed pine and hardwood, and spruce-fir forests. There are also records from mossy rock ledges, and even a few from coniferous bogs and swamps.

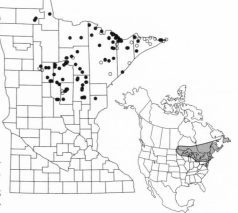

Known flowering dates: June 12-August 26.

Description: Stems 18-33 cm long (including inflorescence), pubescent, arising singly from a branching horizontal rhizome; leaves 3 to 8 per stem, elliptical to ovate or lance-ovate, 2.5-6.5 cm long, 1.2-2.3 cm wide, bluish green with white or pale green reticulation, essentially basal, forming an evergreen rosette; inflorescence a moderately dense spicate raceme, 5.0-17.0 cm long, 1.2-1.6 cm wide, secund, spiraled or cylindrical, consisting of 21 to 45 white flowers; ovaries 3.5-9.0 mm long, 1.5-3.0 mm wide at anthesis; sepals elliptical-oblong to ovate-lanceolate, 3.5-6.3 mm long, 2.0-3.2 mm wide; petals spatulate, 3.5-5.8 mm long, 1.8-2.3 mm wide, connivent with the dorsal sepal to form a hood over the lip; lip globular-saccate, contracted above the middle to form a beak up to 1.5 mm long, entire lip 3.0-4.5 mm long, 3.0-3.5 mm wide.

Aid to identification: Very similar to *G. repens* var. *ophioides*, but typical specimens of *G. tesselata* are larger (rarely less than 20 cm tall) with a longer inflorescence (usually over 6 cm long) and longer leaves that tend to be proportionately narrower and more pointed (at least one leaf on each plant will be 3 cm long or longer). Difficult specimens with character values intermediate between *G. repens* var. *ophioides* and *G. tesselata* are not uncommon. In most of the recent orchid literature these ambiguous specimens are conveniently said to be hybrids, and some experimental evidence supports that conclusion (Kallunki, 1981).

Comments: Adding to the puzzle of spontaneous hybridization between *G. repens* var. *ophioides* and *G. tesselata* is the evidence that *G. tesselata* itself originated during the early post-Pleistocene (sometime within the past 8,000 years) as a hybrid between *G. repens* var. *ophioides* and *G. oblongifolia* (Kallunki, 1976). If this theory is correct, *G. tesselata* has since expanded its range beyond the area where its parents co-occur (*G. oblongifolia* has never been found in Minnesota, but is known from nearby Wisconsin and Ontario) and is now a reproductively stable, if not fully isolated, species.

G. tesselata is probably pollinated by bumblebees (Kallunki, 1981).

The Genus Liparis *Rich.*
(Twayblade orchids)
❧

The name *Liparis* is from the Greek word variously translated as fat, shining, or greasy, in reference to the appearance of the leaves.

About 250 species distributed in tropical and temperate regions worldwide. Only two species are native to North America, both of which occur in Minnesota. Most closely related to *Malaxis*, but quite distinct in general appearance, at least when seen in flower. The flowers are not as eye-catching or persistent as the fruiting capsules, and as a result most of the specimens seen are in the fruiting stage. For this reason the key includes several nonfloral characters.

A Key to the *Liparis* of Minnesota

1. Floral lip pale purple, 8-12 mm long, 6-9 mm wide; pedicels of fruiting capsules 11-18 mm long (pedicels and capsules together 2.3-3.6 cm long); leaves 2.5-8.5 cm wide, the blade averaging about two-and-a-half times longer than wide; a plant of upland forests.

    L. lilifolia

1. Floral lip yellowish green, 4.0-5.5 mm long, 2.2-3.5 mm wide; pedicels of fruiting capsules 3-7 mm long (pedicels and capsules together 1.1-2.0 cm long); leaves 1.0-4.0 cm wide, the blade averaging about four-and-one-fourth times longer than wide; a plant of wetland habitats.

    L. loeselii

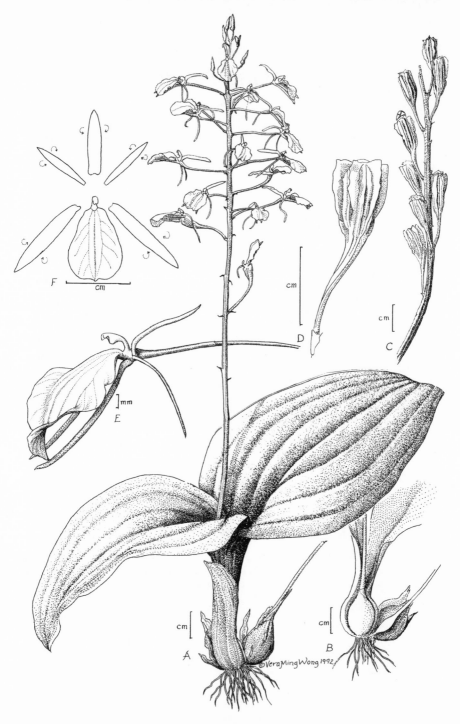

Liparis lilifolia **A**–Flowering plant with pseudobulb of previous season, **B**–Pseudobulbs, longitudinal section, **C**–Infructescence, **D**–Single capsule, **E**–Flower, **F**–Flower, exploded view

Liparis lilifolia (L.) Rich.

Common name: Lily-leaved twayblade.

Abundance: Infrequent.

Habitat: Typically in mature mesic to moist oak or mixed deciduous forests, but in young forests and thickets as well. It also occurs in natural white pine (*Pinus strobus*) stands, and in white pine and red pine (*Pinus resinosa*) plantations. It seems to prefer acidic soil with fairly high organic content.

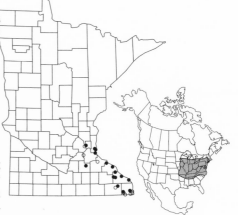

Known flowering dates: June 6-July 7.

Description: Stem 9–25 cm long (including inflorescence), angled and obscurely winged above, glabrous, arising from an ovate pseudobulb (two pseudobulbs typically present; the parent pseudobulb is enveloped in old leaf-bases and connected laterally by a short rhizome to the daughter pseudobulb, which gives rise to the current year's stem, the parent pseudobulb often retaining the dried stem of the previous year); leaves two, basal, sheathing the pseudobulb and the lower part of the stem, elliptical to elliptical-ovate, acute to obtuse, 4.0-16.0 cm long, 2.5-8.5 cm wide; inflorescence a terminal raceme, 4.0-13.0 cm long, 3.0-5.0 cm wide, consisting of 6 to 24 mostly pale purple flowers; ovary and pedicel together 8-14 mm long; capsules oblong to obovate, winged, 1.1-1.8 cm long, 4.0-6.5 mm wide; sepals linear, pale green or yellowish, 8.0-11.5 mm long, 1.2-2.0 mm wide; petals filiform, purple, 8.5-12.0 mm long, about 0.3 mm wide; lip pale purple, obovate, apiculate at apex, 8-12 mm long, 6-9 mm wide.

Aid to identification: Flowering specimens, with their broad purple lip, are quite distinctive and should not be confused with any other Minnesota orchid. Fruiting specimens and specimens with no reproductive structures could be confused with *L. loeselii.* The capsules of *L. lilifolia* have longer pedicels (invariably over 10 mm long) and the leaf blades are proportionately broader (ranging from one-third to two-thirds as wide as long).

Comments: Although typical of mature oak forests, it is occasionally found in thickets of young saplings that only a few years earlier may have been plowed fields. It is even able to colonize pine plantations where the soil is often sandy and relatively sterile. In spite of these pioneering abilities, it remains an infrequent plant and shows no evidence of moving into disturbed habitats beyond its original range.

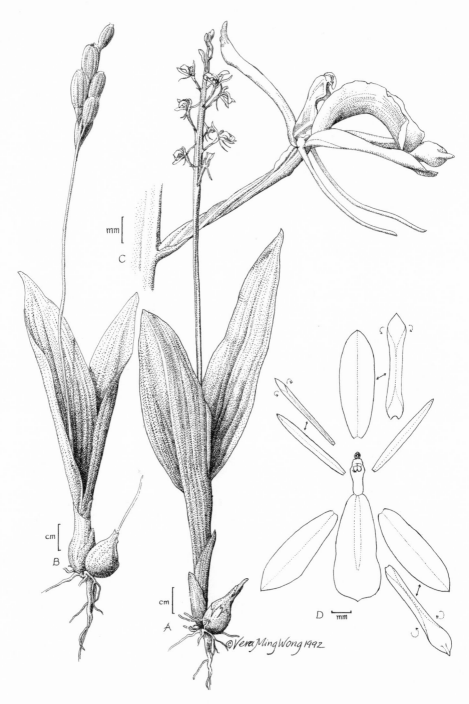

Liparis loeselii **A**–Flowering plant with pseudobulb of previous season, **B**–Fruiting plant, with expanded base forming new pseudobulb, and with pseudobulb of previous season, **C**–Flower, **D**–Flower, exploded view

Liparis loeselii (L.) Rich.

Common name: Loesel's twayblade.

Abundance: Frequent, but easily over-looked.

Habitat: Meadows, fens, swamps, floating mats, pond margins, and sandy lake shores. It occurs in full sunlight or partial shade; usually in peat but occasionally in mineral soil. It tolerates a range of pH values from weakly acidic to strongly calcareous.

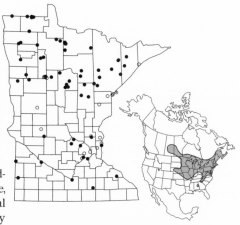

Known flowering dates: June 17-July 29.

Description: Stem 8.5-26.0 cm long (including inflorescence), somewhat angled above, glabrous, arising from an ovate or elliptical pseudobulb (two pseudobulbs typically present; the parent pseudobulb is enveloped in old leaf-bases and connected laterally by a short rhizome to the daughter pseudobulb, which gives rise to the current year's stem, the parent pseudobulb often retaining the dried stem of the previous year); leaves two, basal, sheathing the pseudobulb and the lower part of the stem, elliptical to oblong, acute to obtuse, 3.7-16.0 cm long, 1.0-4.0 cm wide; inflorescence a terminal raceme, 2.5-11.0 cm long, 1.0-2.0 cm wide, consisting of 3 to 19 yellowish green flowers; ovary and pedicel together 4.0-10.0 mm long; capsules obovate to oblong, winged, 9-13 mm long, 4-6 mm wide; sepals oblong-lanceolate, 4.5-6.0 mm long, about 1.0 mm wide; petals filiform, 4.5-5.5 mm long; lip yellowish green, obovate to oblong, apiculate at apex, 4.0-5.5 mm long, 2.2-3.5 mm wide.

Aid to identification: Although not possessing a memorable flower, a normal specimen with flowers or fruit can be easily and reliably keyed to the correct species. Certainly when flowers are present it can be told at a glance from its closest relative, *L. lilifolia*. In fruit they look very similar, but the capsules of *L. loeselii* have shorter pedicels (not exceeding 7 mm in length) and the leaf blades are proportionately narrower (ranging from one-eighth to one-third as wide as long).

Comments: This is one of our most common and widespread orchids. However, it is inconspicuous and rarely occurs in any great numbers, and therefore is often overlooked. It is one of our more widely adapted orchids, occurring in an amazing range of habitats, including a variety of transitional and early-stage successional types. It is also notable for its tolerance of nutrient extremes. For example, in calcareous fens it can be found rooted in marl deposits where the pH may be as high as 8.3.

The Genus Listera R. Br.
(Twayblade orchids)

The name *Listera* is in honor of Martin Lister (1638-1711), an English naturalist.

A small genus of about 25 species occurring in temperate and boreal habitats throughout the Northern Hemisphere. Eight species occur in North America and three in Minnesota. All of our species are small, short-lived plants of cool, northern forests.

A Key to the *Listera* of Minnesota

1. Lip 3.0–5.0 mm long, the apex cleft at least one-half the length of the lip, producing two linear-lanceolate pointed lobes; column very short and inconspicuous, about 0.5 mm long.

L. cordata

1. Lip 7.0–12.0 mm long, the apex merely notched, or at most cleft one-third the length of the lip, producing two broadly rounded lobes; column conspicuous, 2.5–3.5 mm long.

   2. Lip with broad basal auricles that clasp the column, the base nearly as broad as the apex, the apex notched one-fifth to one-third of the length of the lip; pedicels and ovaries smooth, not glandular.

L. auriculata

   2. Lip without basal auricles, although lateral "bumps" are present about one-fourth of the way up from the base, otherwise the lip tapers more or less evenly from apex to base, the apex notched one-tenth to one-fifth of the length of the lip; pedicels and ovaries distinctly glandular.

L. convallarioides

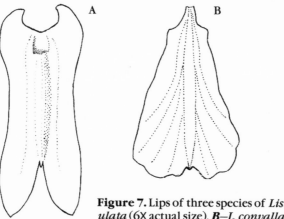

Figure 7. Lips of three species of *Listera: A—L. auriculata* (6X actual size), *B—L. convallarioides* (4X), *C—L. cordata* (5X)

*Although inhospitable to humans, floating "bogs"
provide ideal habitat for many rare orchids.*

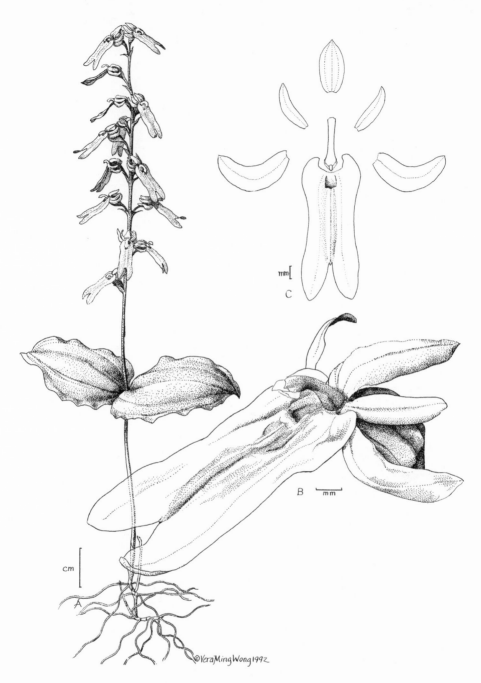

Listera auriculata **A**–Flowering plant, **B**–Flower, **C**–Flower, exploded view

Listera auriculata Wieg.

Common name: Auricled twayblade.

Abundance: Very rare. Listed as endangered in Minnesota. Report all sightings to the Minnesota DNR.

Habitat: Characteristically along streams in low, moist hardwood forests, mixed hardwood-coniferous forests, and shrub swamps. These are typically shady, mossy, acidic habitats on alluvial deposits or shallow organic soil.

Known flowering dates: June 20-July 11.

Description: Stem 9-18 cm long (including inflorescence), pubescent above the leaves, glabrous below; roots few, fibrous; leaves two per stem, subopposite, sessile, ovate to elliptical, attached near the middle of the stem, 2.7-5.0 cm long, 2.1-3.6 cm wide; inflorescence a terminal raceme, 4.0-7.5 cm long, 2.0-2.5 cm wide, consisting of 8 to 16 pale green flowers; pedicels 2.5-5.0 mm long, glabrous; ovaries 3.0-4.5 mm long, 1.8-2.8 mm wide at anthesis, glabrous; sepals elliptical to ovate or oblong to obovate, 3.2-4.5 mm long, 1.0-1.5 mm wide, the lateral sepals somewhat longer and proportionately narrower than the dorsal sepal and distinctly falcate; petals linear to linear-oblong, 3.0-3.7 mm long, about 0.8 mm wide; lip obovate to oblong or nearly rectangular, 7.0-10.0 mm long, 2.0-5.0 mm wide at the widest point (usually the apex), margins minutely ciliate, apex cleft or notched approximately one-fifth to one-third the length of the lip, producing two broadly rounded lobes, the base with auricles curving around and clasping the base of the column; column 2.5-3.3 mm long, dilated at summit and curving downward.

Aid to identification: *L. auriculata* is most likely to be confused with *L. convallarioides,* but the lip of *L. auriculata* has a broad base, nearly as broad as the tip, and the pedicels and ovaries are smooth, without glands. In contrast, the lip of *L. convallarioides* narrows distinctly near the base, and the pedicels and ovaries are densely glandular.

Putative hybrids between *L. auriculata* and *L. convallarioides* (named *L. Xveltmanii* Case) have been found in Wisconsin, Michigan, Ontario, and elsewhere, but not yet in Minnesota. Such hybrids possess characteristics intermediate between the two parents (Catling, 1976).

Comments: This rare and enigmatic orchid has intrigued Minnesota botanists since it was first discovered in the state over one hundred years ago. Its elusive nature and seemingly capricious choice of habitats have frustrated all attempts to study its natural history. What little we can glean from the collection record would tend to support its reputation for occurring in rather small, transient colonies; however, only two of the five records have reliable population counts, and none has a history of observation greater than six years.

Listera convallarioides **A**–Flowering plant, in two portions, **B**–Flower, **C**–
Flower, exploded view

Listera convallarioides (Sw.) Nutt.

Common name: Broad-leaved twayblade.

Abundance: Very rare; known in Minnesota by a single herbarium specimen collected somewhere near Mineral Center (Cook County) in 1924.

Habitat: The only Minnesota specimen was collected from a habitat described as a "cedar-spruce-balsam forest." This description implies a weakly acidic swamp, probably with a ground cover of *Sphagnum* moss.

Known flowering dates: The single Minnesota specimen was collected in flower bud on July 5.

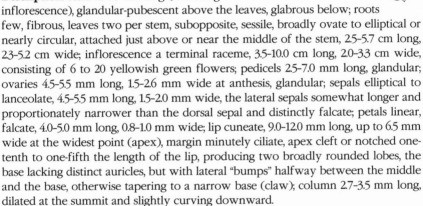

Description: Stem 11-27 cm long (including inflorescence), glandular-pubescent above the leaves, glabrous below; roots few, fibrous, leaves two per stem, subopposite, sessile, broadly ovate to elliptical or nearly circular, attached just above or near the middle of the stem, 2.5-5.7 cm long, 2.3-5.2 cm wide; inflorescence a terminal raceme, 3.5-10.0 cm long, 2.0-3.3 cm wide, consisting of 6 to 20 yellowish green flowers; pedicels 2.5-7.0 mm long, glandular; ovaries 4.5-5.5 mm long, 1.5-2.6 mm wide at anthesis, glandular; sepals elliptical to lanceolate, 4.5-5.5 mm long, 1.5-2.0 mm wide, the lateral sepals somewhat longer and proportionately narrower than the dorsal sepal and distinctly falcate; petals linear, falcate, 4.0-5.0 mm long, 0.8-1.0 mm wide; lip cuneate, 9.0-12.0 mm long, up to 6.5 mm wide at the widest point (apex), margin minutely ciliate, apex cleft or notched one-tenth to one-fifth the length of the lip, producing two broadly rounded lobes, the base lacking distinct auricles, but with lateral "bumps" halfway between the middle and the base, otherwise tapering to a narrow base (claw); column 2.7-3.5 mm long, dilated at the summit and slightly curving downward.

Aid to identification: *L. convallarioides* looks superficially similar to *L. auriculata*, but the lip of *L. convallarioides* is broad at the tip and narrow at the base whereas the lip of *L. auriculata* is nearly as broad at the base as at the tip. Also, the pedicels and ovaries are distinctly glandular in *L. convallarioides* (as seen under 10X magnification), but without glands in *L. auriculata*.

Reported to hybridize with *L. auriculata*, producing an offspring with intermediate characters (Catling, 1976).

Comments: Given the lack of recent records it is tempting to declare this species extinct in Minnesota. However, a large amount of potential habitat (as much as one million acres) is essentially unexplored by botanists. It seems likely that in time *L. convallarioides* will be rediscovered. With that goal in mind, it would be well worth the time of any adventurous botanist to explore the coniferous forests and swamps of northeastern Minnesota.

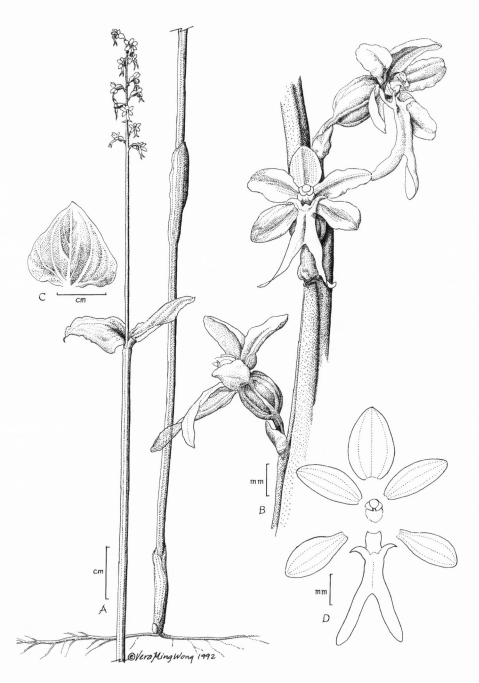

Listera cordata **A**–Flowering plant, in two portions, **B**–Portion of inflorescence,
C–Leaf, **D**–Flower, exploded view

Listera cordata (L.) R. Br.

Common name: Heart-leaved twayblade.

Abundance: Frequent in the northeast, occasional elsewhere, but easily overlooked.

Habitat: It typically occurs on *Sphagnum* hummocks in coniferous bogs and swamps, but is also found in upland forests (both coniferous and hardwood) where it may grow in humus or needle duff.

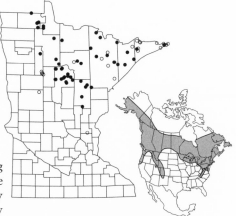

Known flowering dates: June 8-August 5.

Description: Stems 11–33 cm long (including inflorescence), glandular-pubescent above the leaves, glabrous below, arising singly from long creeping rhizomes; roots few and fibrous; leaves two per stem, opposite, sessile, ovate-deltate, attached near the middle of the stem, 1.0–3.9 cm long, 0.9–3.3 cm wide; inflorescence a terminal raceme, 2.0–13.0 cm long, 0.8–1.9 cm wide, consisting of 6 to 21 minute green or more often reddish purple flowers; pedicels 1.2–2.5 mm long, glabrous; ovaries nearly globular, 2.0–4.2 mm long and 1.2–3.0 mm wide at anthesis; sepals ovate-elliptical to oblong, 1.5–2.8 mm long, 0.8–1.0 mm wide; petals similar but somewhat smaller; lip linear-oblong, 3.0–5.0 mm long, with a narrow tooth on each side near the base; the apex cleft at least one-half the length of the lip, producing two parallel or slightly divergent linear-lanceolate lobes; column short and stout, about 0.5 mm long.

Aid to identification: All the *Listera*s have two broad, flat, opposite leaves attached near the middle of the stem (hence the common name). This characteristic alone separates the *Listera*s from all similar-looking orchids. Among the *Listera*s, *L. cordata* is distinguished by its deeply forked lip; the others have lips notched only at the tip. Although the lip is very small, the shape can usually be seen without magnification.

Comments: This is one of the most wide ranging of all orchids. It occurs across northern Europe and Asia as well as transcontinentally in North America. It is relatively common in parts of Minnesota, often occurring in large numbers (especially in cedar swamps), but because of its small size and pale color it is easily overlooked. It seems that the individual plants are relatively short-lived and may not persist for more than a few years. Even established colonies seem rather unstable and are prone to unpredictable expansions and contractions.

A curious feature of the biology of this species is the speed with which the seeds ripen. The ovaries often split and shed mature seeds even before the flowers wither.

It is known to be pollinated by fungus gnats, but it is probably pollinated by a number of other small insects as well (Ackerman and Mesler, 1979).

The Genus Malaxis *Sw.* (*Adder's-mouth orchids*)

The name *Malaxis* is from the Greek word meaning soft or delicate, in apparent reference to the leaves.

About 200 to 250 species worldwide, nine in North America, three in Minnesota. Possessing the smallest flowers of any Minnesota orchid, and among the smallest of any orchid known. Floral characters are not emphasized in the key because of the difficulty in seeing and measuring critical details of floral morphology, especially in pressed specimens.

A Key to the *Malaxis* of Minnesota

1. Leaves two or more per stem, basal, less than 2.5 cm long (generally less than 2.0 cm) and not more than 1.0 cm wide.

    M. paludosa

1. Leaf one per stem, the blade appearing to be attached well above the base of the stem, 2.5 cm long or longer and more than 1.0 cm wide.

    2. Inflorescence usually more than 5 cm long (range 4.0-11.5 cm) and less than 1.0 cm wide; flowers evenly spaced within the inflorescence; the longest pedicels no more than 3.0 mm long; floral lip with a narrow pointed apex and dilated base.

        M. monophyllos var. *brachypoda*

    2. Inflorescence usually less than 5 cm long (range 1.5-6.0 cm) and at least 1.0 cm wide; flowers mostly crowded near the summit of the inflorescence with the lower ones more widely spaced; the longest pedicels (the lower ones) 3-8 mm long; floral lip with a wide, blunt, three-toothed apex, not dilated at base.

        M. unifolia

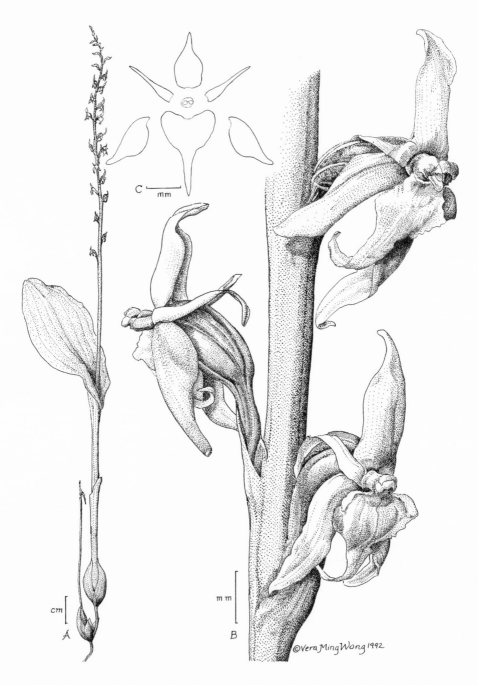

Malaxis monophyllos var. *brachypoda* **A**–Flowering plant, **B**–Portion of inflorescence, **C**–Flower, exploded view

Malaxis monophyllos (L.) Sw. var. *brachypoda* (Gray) Morris & Eames

Synonym: *Malaxis brachypoda* (Gray) Fern.

Common name: White adder's-mouth.

Abundance: Apparently rare or uncommon, but easily overlooked.

Habitat: Typically on *Sphagnum* hummocks in coniferous swamps, under white cedar (*Thuja occidentalis*), black spruce (*Picea mariana*), or tamarack (*Larix laricina*). Also found growing in peat soil in hardwood swamps.

Known flowering dates: June 20-July 29.

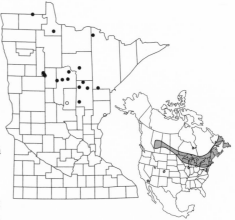

Description: Stem 11-22 cm long (including inflorescence), glabrous, arising from a globular pseudobulb; roots few, fibrous; leaf one per stem, the base strongly sheathing, the blade appearing to be attached above the base of the stem (rarely basal), ovate-elliptical, 2.7-8.0 cm long, 1.3-3.7 cm wide; inflorescence a terminal raceme, forming a relatively long slender spike, 4.0-11.5 cm long, 0.4-0.9 cm wide, consisting of 14 to 34 minute greenish white flowers evenly spaced within the inflorescence; floral bracts lanceolate, 1.0-2.0 mm long; pedicels 1.0-3.0 mm long, the upper and lower ones of approximately equal length; sepals linear to lanceolate or oblong, 1.7-2.5 mm long, 0.5-0.7 mm wide; petals linear, reflexed, 1.5-2.0 mm long, about 0.2 mm wide; lip somewhat triangular, contracted near the middle to produce a narrow lanceolate tip, dilated at the base, with basal auricles curving forward (not easily seen in pressed specimens), 1.4-2.0 mm long, 1.0-1.7 mm wide at base.

Aid to identification: *M. monophyllos* var. *brachypoda* superficially resembles *Listera cordata*, but *L. cordata* has two leaves and *M. monophyllos* var. *brachypoda* has only one. It could also be confused with *M. paludosa* but again is distinguished by its relatively large single leaf. Positive identification of an immature specimen could be difficult if the flower spike had not yet developed. Such a specimen would closely resemble *M. unifolia*.

Identification could also be difficult if the position of the single leaf is misinterpreted. The critical distinction is the point where the leaf blade diverges from the stem, not where the leaf sheath is attached. In *M. monophyllos* var. *brachypoda* that point is well above the base of the stem; in *M. paludosa* that point is at the base.

Comments: *M. monophyllos* var. *brachypoda* differs from the typical variety found in Europe in that its flowers are twisted 180° instead of 360°.

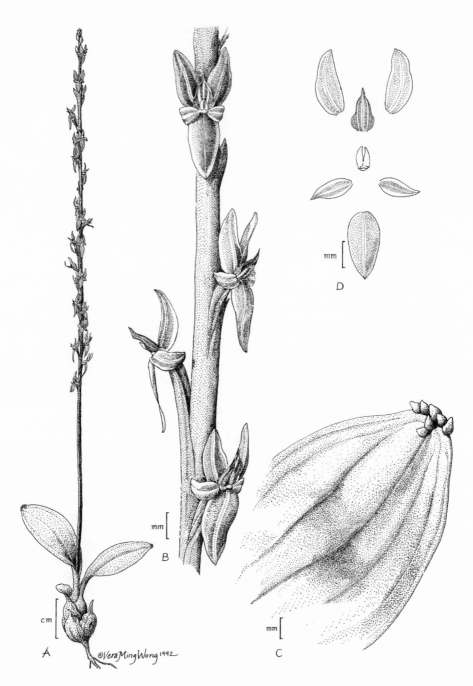

Malaxis paludosa *A*–Flowering plant, *B*–Portion of inflorescence, *C*–Leaf with marginal foliar embryos, *D*–Flower, exploded view

Malaxis paludosa (L.) Sw.

Synonym: *Hammarbya paludosa* (L.) O. Kuntze.

Common name: Bog adder's-mouth.

Abundance: Very rare. Listed as endangered in Minnesota. Report all sightings to the Minnesota DNR.

Habitat: All known occurrences are in black spruce (*Picea mariana*) swamps, where the plants grow perched on hummocks of *Sphagnum* or rarely *Mnium* moss. Other types of swamps and bogs may also provide suitable habitat.

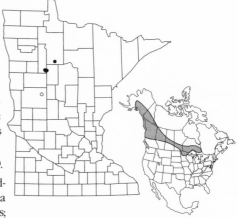

Known flowering dates: July 11-August 29.

Description: Stem 7.5-15.0 cm long (including inflorescence), glabrous, arising from a globular pseudobulb; roots few, fibrous; leaves 2 to 5 per stem, basal, elliptical to obovate, 1.0-1.8 cm long (extreme specimens with leaves to 2.5 cm long), 0.3-1.0 cm wide, sheathing at base, often with marginal foliar embryos toward tip; inflorescence a terminal raceme, 2.7-9.0 cm long, 4-7 mm wide, consisting of 10 to 29 minute greenish yellow flowers evenly spaced within the inflorescence; flowers twisted 360° so that the lip is uppermost of the perianth parts; floral bracts lanceolate, 2.0-3.0 mm long; pedicels to 2.5 mm long; sepals ovate-lanceolate to elliptical, 2.0-3.0 mm long, 1.0-1.4 mm wide; petals ovate-lanceolate, 1.0-1.5 mm long, about 0.5 mm wide; lip variable, ovate, sometimes with a noticeable constriction above the middle producing a "nipple" at the apex, rarely with a second constriction below the first, resulting in a vague three-lobed appearance, 1.7-1.9 mm long, about 0.8 mm wide at the widest point.

Aid to identification: *Malaxis monophyllos* var. *brachypoda* is superficially similar, but has only one leaf, which is relatively large and appears to be attached well above the base of the stem. In contrast, *M. paludosa* has two or more leaves that are much smaller and are attached at the base of the stem.

Comments: The challenge presented by this amazing plant is not in identifying it, but in finding it in the first place. It is without a doubt the smallest and most inconspicuous orchid in Minnesota. For this reason it is easily overlooked, even when one is searching on hands and knees. This has given it the reputation as one of the rarest orchids in North America (Baldwin, 1961). It also occurs in Eurasia, where it seems to be less rare, or at least more often found (Summerhayes, 1951).

A curious adaptation of this plant is its ability to produce tiny foliar embryos at the margins of its leaves. When these embryos are dislodged or when the leaf falls to the ground, the embryos can develop directly into adult plants (Taylor, 1967).

The only insect that has been observed carrying pollen of this species is a male specimen of the fungus gnat, *Phronia digitata* Heckman (Reeves and Reeves, 1984).

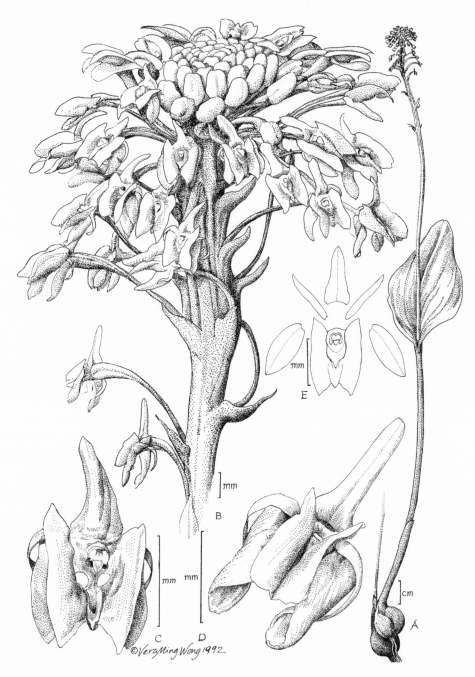

Malaxis unifolia **A**–Flowering plant, **B**–Inflorescence, **C**–Flower, fully open, **D**–Flower, partially open, **E**–Flower, exploded view

Malaxis unifolia Michx.

Common name: Green adder's-mouth.

Abundance: Occasional to locally frequent in the north; rare but probably underreported in the south.

Habitat: Mostly on *Sphagnum* hummocks in coniferous swamps and bogs, but also in sedge meadows, hardwood and shrub swamps, and in upland hardwood and pine forests (including plantations). There are also authentic specimens from lichen-encrusted rock outcrops.

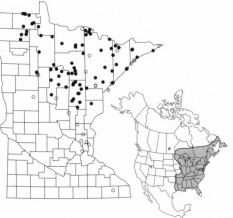

Known flowering dates: June 20-August 22.

Description: Stem 9-29 cm long (including inflorescence), glabrous, arising from a globular pseudobulb; roots few, fibrous; leaf one per stem, the base strongly sheathing, the blade attached near the middle of the stem (clearly not basal), ovate to nearly elliptical, 2.5-7.5 cm long, 1.3-4.0 cm wide; inflorescence a terminal raceme, typically cylindrical or club-shaped, but sometimes fan-shaped or even subcapitate, 1.5-6.0 cm long (extreme examples to 8.0 cm long), 0.7-1.8 cm wide, consisting of 24 to 84 minute green flowers, mostly crowded near the summit with the lower ones more widely spaced; flowers twisted 180° so that the lip is lowermost; floral bracts subulate to triangular, 1.0-5.5 mm long, the lower ones generally longer and proportionately narrower than the upper ones; pedicels 2-3 mm long on the upper flowers, 3-8 mm long on the lower; sepals linear-oblong, about 1.5 mm long, 0.7 mm wide; petals linear, recurved, about 1.5 mm long; lip about 2 mm long, 1.5 mm wide, rectangular to truncate-cordate, with three teeth at the apex, the middle tooth much smaller than the lateral teeth, the base with rounded or pointed auricles.

Aid to identification: The strongest visual impression of *M. unifolia* is of the numerous tiny green flowers clustered near the top of the stem. This effect is most pronounced early in the growing season; by the end of the season the inflorescence will have elongated somewhat. In both *M. monophyllos* var. *brachypoda* and *M. paludosa* the flowers are less numerous and more evenly spaced along the stem. Immature specimens in which the spikes have not yet developed could be difficult to distinguish from *M. monophyllos* var. *brachypoda*.

Comments: This is the most common and widespread *Malaxis* in Minnesota, but it can be difficult to find because of its small size and pale green color. The individual flowers are the smallest of any orchid in Minnesota—so small, in fact, that as many as 50 flowers may be clustered at the tip of the stem in an area the size of a thimble.

The Genus Platanthera *Rich (Rein orchids)*

The name *Platanthera* is from the Greek words meaning "wide anther," a morphological feature of the genus.

Our species had generally been included in the polymorphic genus *Habenaria*, but the current trend is to consider them distinct based on a number of technical characters of the flowers, the most definitive being the absence of stigmatic processes. Following this example true *Habenaria* are strictly tropical and subtropical and *Platanthera* strictly temperate. There are about 200 species of *Platanthera* worldwide, including 36 in North America and 10 in Minnesota. The *Platanthera* constitute the largest genus of orchids in the state, including the most abundant species and the rarest.

A Key to the *Platanthera* of Minnesota

1. Lip more than 5 mm wide, deeply divided into three lobes, at least the lateral lobes distinctly fringed.

    2. Flowers white or greenish white, lateral lobes of lip cut more than halfway to the base, producing individual fringe segments more than 2 mm long.

        3. Lip 2.0–3.8 cm wide (when flattened); spur 3.5–6.0 cm long; inflorescence 5.0–9.0 cm wide; petals fan-shaped, 10–17 mm long.

P. praeclara

        3. Lip 0.5–1.9 cm wide; spur 1.1–1.7 cm long; inflorescence 2.0–4.5 cm wide; petals more or less linear, 2.8–6.0 mm long.

P. lacera

    2. Flowers purple, lobes of lip cut less than halfway to the base, producing individual fringe segments 2 mm long or less.

P. psycodes

1. Lip less than 5 mm wide, not divided into three lobes, not fringed.

    4. Leaves cauline, the stem bearing one or more fully developed leaves.

        5. Leaf one, attached somewhat below the middle of the stem (1 to 3 reduced bractlike leaves usually present above the principal leaf); inflorescence less than 5 cm long, usually with fewer than 18 flowers (range: 5–20); the largest floral bracts (usually the lowest) less than 12 mm long; spur about 10 mm long (about twice as long as the lip).

P. clavellata

        5. Leaves 2 to 6, the uppermost often attached at or above the middle of the stem (there may also be 1 to 3 reduced bractlike leaves above the principal leaves); inflorescence more than 5 cm long, often with more than 18 flowers (range: 10–65); the largest floral bracts 12 mm long or longer; spur less than 8 mm long.

            6. Lip ovate, the apex scalloped or shallowly toothed, a conspicuous tubercle rising vertically from near the base.

P. flava

            6. Lip prolonged into a linear-lanceolate tip without a scalloped or toothed apex, and without a tubercle near the base.

                7. Flowers white when fresh, becoming light straw colored or pale brown when dried; lip abruptly dilated at base.

P. dilatata

7. Flowers green or yellowish green when fresh, becoming yellowish green to brown when dried; lip not abruptly dilated at base, instead tapering more or less evenly from base to tip.

P. hyperborea

4. Principal leaves basal, the stem bearing at most only vestigial bractlike leaves.

8. Leaf one (occasionally a much reduced bractlike leaf occurring between the principal leaf and the inflorescence), obovate; spur less than 1 cm long; lip less than 7.0 mm long.

P. obtusata

8. Leaves two, opposite elliptical to orbicular; spur more than 1 cm long; lip more than 7.0 mm long.

9. Stem with 1 to 6 bracts scattered below the inflorescence; spur slightly thickened toward the tip; lip blunt or rounded at apex; dorsal sepal 3.5-6.0 mm long and about as wide; ovaries on apparent pedicels 4-10 mm long.

P. orbiculata

9. Stem without bracts below the inflorescence; spur about the same width throughout or more often narrowed toward the tip; lip acute or acuminate at apex; dorsal sepal 6.0-10.0 mm long and about one-half as wide; ovaries apparently sessile.

P. hookeri

Platanthera clavellata **A**–Flowering plant, **B**–Inflorescence, **C**–Portion of inflorescence, **D**–Flower, exploded view

Platanthera clavellata (Michx.) Luer

Synonym: *Habenaria clavellata* (Michx.) Spreng.

Common name: Small green wood-orchid.

Abundance: Uncommon to rare.

Habitat: Mostly in boreal-type *Sphagnum* swamps and floating mats; usually associated with scattered, often stunted black spruce (*Picea mariana*) or tamarack (*Larix laricina*). There is also a record from an acid peaty meadow on the Anoka Sandplain.

Known flowering dates: July 11-July 30.

Description: Stem 15-33 cm long (including inflorescence), glabrous; roots slender and fleshy; principal leaf one, attached some-

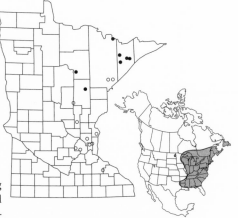

what below the middle of the stem (1 to 3 vestigial bractlike leaves usually present above the principal leaf), obovate to oblanceolate or oblong, 5.0-14.0 cm long, 1.0-2.8 cm wide; inflorescence a short terminal raceme, 1.5-4.5 cm long, 1.5-2.5 cm wide, consisting of 5 to 20 greenish yellow flowers; floral bracts to 1.1 cm long; ovaries 5.5-10.0 mm long, 1.3-2.5 mm wide at anthesis; sepals ovate, 2.0-4.5 mm long, 1.5-2.7 mm wide; petals similar to the sepals; lip oblong, shallowly toothed at apex, 2.5-5.5 mm long, 1.5-2.5 mm wide; spur club-shaped (clavate), 9-11 mm long.

Aid to identification: This species is superficially similar to *P. obtusata*. They are both small green swamp orchids, and share the feature of only one principal leaf. In *P. clavellata* the leaf is attached somewhere near or just below the middle of the stem, and in *P. obtusata* the leaf is attached at the very base of the stem. In swamp habitats the point where the leaf is attached may be hidden below the surface of the living *Sphagnum*, making it necessary to separate the moss carefully to find the base of the plant.

Comments: The collection record indicates that at one time *P. clavellata* may have been common in the metropolitan counties, but in the early twentieth century it began to decline as its habitats were destroyed or degraded by urban activities. At the present time there are no sites known to survive in southern or central Minnesota, and only a few in the north. Still, it is likely that one or more colonies survive in the south and await discovery by the determined (or lucky) orchid hunter.

In living specimens the flowers often have a peculiar crooked appearance. This results from the flowers' twisting somewhat less or more than the expected 180°.

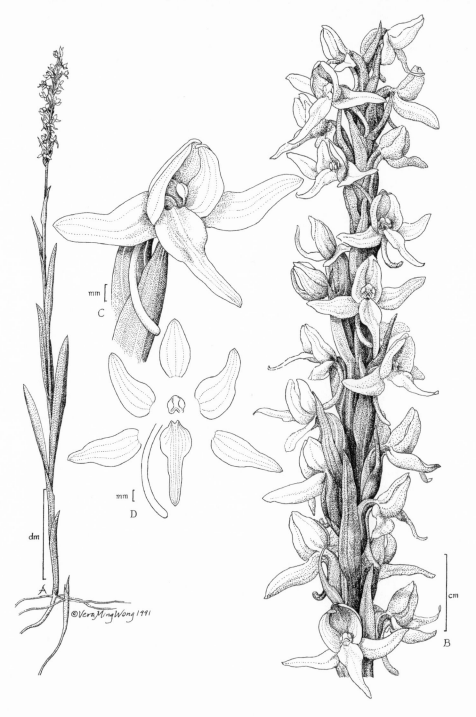

Platanthera dilatata *A*–Flowering plant, ***B***–Inflorescence, ***C***–Flower, ***D***–Flower, exploded view

Platanthera dilatata (Pursh) Lindl. ex Beck

Synonym: *Habenaria dilatata* (Pursh) Hook.

Common name: Tall white bog-orchid.

Abundance: Infrequent to occasional.

Habitat: Moderately to weakly acidic to circumneutral coniferous/*Sphagnum* swamps, floating mats, muskeg, and sedge meadows. These are typically late-stage successional plant communities in relatively undisturbed habitats.

Known flowering dates: July 4-August 31.

Description: Stem 36-75 cm long (including inflorescence), glabrous; roots fleshy; principal leaves 3 to 6 per stem (with an additional 1 or 2 vestigial bractlike leaves above the principal leaves), cauline, lanceolate or

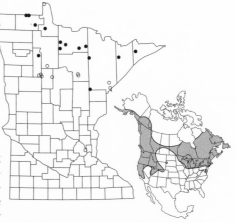

linear to narrowly elliptical, 8-20 cm long, 0.7-2.0 cm wide; inflorescence a terminal raceme, 5-23 cm long, consisting of 10 to 60 white flowers (drying whitish, straw-colored, or pale brown); floral bracts 0.7-2.7 cm long; ovaries 7.0-11.0 mm long, 2.3-4.0 mm wide at anthesis; dorsal sepal ovate-elliptical, 3.3-7.3 mm long, 2.0-3.0 mm wide; lateral sepals lanceolate to narrowly elliptical, 4.0-9.0 mm long, 1.0-3.0 mm wide; petals similar in size and general shape to the sepals, but asymmetrical and falcate, dilated at base, connivent with dorsal sepal to form a vague hood over the column (not usually discernible in pressed specimens); lip linear-lanceolate, abruptly dilated at base, 5.0-8.0 mm long, 1.0-3.3 mm wide; spur 4.5-7.7 mm long.

Aid to identification: Living specimens exhibit brilliant white and fragrant flowers, but otherwise closely resemble *P. hyperborea*. The flowers usually fade when dried; the only reliable way to tell them apart then is by the shape of the lip. The lip of *P. hyperborea* is very narrow and evenly tapered from the base to the tip; the lip of *P. dilatata* is the same basic shape, but the base is dilated, producing a distinct "bulge."

Some specimens appear intermediate between *P. dilatata* and *P. hyperborea* and are presumably hybrids. These hybrids have been named *P. ✕media* (Rydb.) Luer (Luer, 1975) and are fairly common in Minnesota.

Comments: The dense spike of pure white flowers can appear almost luminescent against the often drab background of its wetland habitat, inspiring the alternative common name of bog candles.

Pollinated by bees (*Hymenoptera*), and moths and butterflies (*Lepidoptera*) (Stoutamire, 1968).

Platanthera flava **A**–Flowering plant, **B**–Portion of inflorescence, **C**–Flowers, **D**–Flower, exploded view

Platanthera flava (L.) Lindl. var. *herbiola* (R. Br.) Luer

Synonym: *Habenaria flava* (L.) R. Br. var. *herbiola* (R. Br.) Ames & Correll.

Common name: Tubercled rein-orchid.

Abundance: Very rare. Listed as endangered in Minnesota. Report all sightings to the Minnesota DNR.

Habitat: Moist grassy or sedge-dominated meadows on calcareous or circumneutral substrata. The known habitats tend to be somewhat brushy, with scattered willow (*Salix*) and dogwood (*Cornus*).

Known flowering dates: July 3–July 24.

Description: Stem 17–45 cm long (including inflorescence), glabrous; principal leaves 2 to 4 per stem (with an additional 1 to 3 vestigial bractlike leaves above the principal

leaves), cauline, lanceolate to ovate-lanceolate or elliptical, the bases strongly sheathing the stem, 5.0–15.0 cm long, 1.5–4.5 cm wide; inflorescence a terminal raceme, 5.0–12.0 cm long, 1.5–2.0 cm wide, consisting of 14 to 53 greenish flowers; floral bracts 0.8–2.7 cm long; ovaries 6.0–8.0 mm long, 1.2–1.5 mm wide at anthesis; sepals ovate, 2.0–3.2 mm long, 1.5–2.1 mm wide; petals similar to sepals; lip ovate, 2.7–3.8 mm long, 1.3–3.3 mm wide, with a tooth on each side near the base and a single prominent tubercle rising vertically from the floor of the lip near the base, the margin at apex scalloped or shallowly toothed; spur 4.5–5.5 mm long.

Aid to identification: Superficially similar to the common *P. hyperborea*, which may occur in the same habitat. The surest way to distinguish *P. flava* var. *herbiola* is by the distinctive tubercle at the base of the lip. It appears as a relatively prominent bump and can be seen without magnification.

All our specimens, as described here, are var. *herbiola* (R. Br.) Luer. They differ from specimens of the more southerly var. *flava* in their longer floral bracts, a proportionately narrower lip, and a leafier stem.

Comments: The peculiar tubercle at the base of the lip apparently functions to deflect pollinators (mosquitoes and moths) toward one of the two pollinia, which adhere to the proboscis and may later be deposited on the stigma of another flower (Stoutamire, 1968).

P. flava var. *herbiola* is somewhat enigmatic. It occurs over a relatively large portion of Minnesota, yet there are so few records. Its distribution is probably controlled by specific habitat requirements as well as historical factors. In any case, it presents the orchid hunter with a unique challenge.

Platanthera hookeri **A**–Flowering plant, **B**–Portion of inflorescence, **C**–Flower, **D**–Flower, exploded view

Platanthera hookeri (Torr.) Lindl.

Synonym: *Habenaria hookeri* Torr. ex Gray.

Common name: Hooker's orchid.

Abundance: Occasional in the north, infrequent or rare in the south.

Habitat: In northern Minnesota it typically occurs in upland pine forests, and less often in coniferous swamps. In southern Minnesota it is found in mesic deciduous forests (usually on north-facing slopes).

Known flowering dates: June 3-July 25.

Description: Stem 19-45 cm long (including inflorescence), glabrous; roots fleshy; leaves two per stem, opposite, basal, elliptical to orbicular, 5.5-15.0 cm long, 4.0-10.5 cm wide,

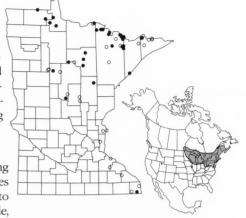

widely spreading and more or less lying on the ground; cauline bracts absent; inflorescence a terminal raceme, 8-23 cm long, 2.5-4.5 cm wide, consisting of 6 to 27 yellowish green flowers; floral bracts 1.1-2.1 cm long; ovaries 1.0-1.3 cm long, 1.0-2.5 mm wide at anthesis, essentially sessile; dorsal sepal ovate, somewhat connivent with petals to form a vague hood over the lip (not easily recognized in pressed specimens), 6.0-10.0 mm long, 3.0-5.0 mm wide; lateral sepals narrowly oblong, 7.5-11.0 mm long, 2.0-3.7 mm wide; petals linear-lanceolate, curved (falcate), 5.0-7.5 mm long, 1.1-1.5 mm wide at the widest point; lip entire, lanceolate, with an acute tip, 7.5-13.0 mm long, 1.6-5.0 mm wide; spur 1.2-2.1 cm long, more or less a constant width throughout or often narrowing near the tip.

Aid to identification: Similar in general appearance to the larger *P. orbiculata*. Both have large, flat, roundish leaves that lie more or less flat on the ground. The two can be distinguished by several technical differences in flower structure, but an easy and reliable way to tell them apart is by the presence of bracts on the stem of *P. orbiculata* and their absence on *P. hookeri*. The shape of the spur is also a good field character: in *P. hookeri* it generally tapers to a point, but in *P. orbiculata* it is thickened at the tip like a club.

Comments: *P. hookeri* is not particularly uncommon in the northern part of the state, where it occurs in a variety of habitats throughout the coniferous forest zone. (The apparent gap in Beltrami and Koochiching counties reflects a lack of looking there.) The situation is different in southern Minnesota, where *P. hookeri* legitimately seems rare. It is also more ecologically restrained in the south, where it is limited to cool microhabitats in areas of extreme topographical relief, such as the St. Croix Valley and the steep valleys of the Paleozoic Plateau.

Platanthera hyperborea **A**–Flowering plant, **B**–Portion of inflorescence, **C**–Flower, exploded view

Platanthera hyperborea (L.) Lindl.

Synonym: *Habenaria hyperborea* (L.) R. Br.

Common name: Northern bog-orchid.

Abundance: Relatively common.

Habitat: Meadows, marshes, swales, fens, bogs, swamps, shrub swamps, thickets, and shores; in shade or full sunlight; in peat or mineral soil. Sometimes associated with early-stage successional plant communities.

Known flowering dates: June 16-August 16.

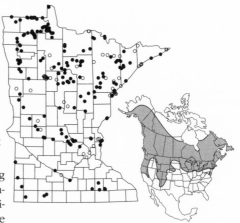

Description: Stem 19-87 cm long (including inflorescence), glabrous; roots fleshy; principal leaves 2 to 7 per stem (with an additional 1 to 3 vestigial bractlike leaves above the principal leaves), cauline, oblong to linear or narrowly elliptical, 7-30 cm long, 1.5-5.0 cm wide; inflorescence a terminal raceme, 4-25 cm long, consisting of 13 to 65 greenish flowers (drying yellowish green to brown); floral bracts 0.6-2.8 cm long; ovaries 6.5-14.0 mm long, 2.8-4.0 mm wide at anthesis; dorsal sepal ovate-elliptical, 2.8-6.0 mm long, 1.8-3.0 mm wide; lateral sepals similar but somewhat longer and proportionately narrower; petals about as long as the sepals, ovate-lanceolate, asymmetrical and falcate, dilated at base, connivent with dorsal sepal to form a vague hood over the column (not usually discernible in pressed specimens); lip lanceolate, not abruptly dilated at base, 3.0-6.0 mm long, 0.8-2.2 mm wide; spur 2.5-6.5 mm long.

Aid to identification: Very similar to *P. dilatata*, but living specimens can be easily distinguished by flower color (white in *P. dilatata*; greenish in *P. hyperborea*). In herbarium specimens the color often fades, and flowers of both species may appear pale yellowish brown. In this case, the shape of the lip is the only reliable distinguishing character (see dichotomy 7 of the *Platanthera* key). The two species can, however, hybridize and produce offspring with intermediate characteristics (*P. ×media* (Rydb.) Luer).

P. flava also appears similar, and has greenish flowers, but it has a distinctively shaped lip that includes a prominent tubercle near the base, which can be seen without magnification.

Specimens taller than 40 cm and with more than six leaves have been segregated as var. *huronensis* (Nutt.) Luer. This variety is not uncommon in Minnesota and often occurs with the typical variety. However, the value of distinguishing this variety is questionable.

Comments: This is probably the most abundant and frequently encountered orchid in Minnesota. It is capable of colonizing an amazing array of habitat types, including a wide range of pH values from moderately acidic to strongly calcareous.

Stoutamire (1968) reports that it is probably pollinated by mosquitoes.

Platanthera lacera **A**–Flowering plant, **B**–Inflorescence, **C**–Flower, **D**–Flower, exploded view

Platanthera lacera (Michx.) G. Don

Synonym: *Habenaria lacera* (Michx.) Lodd.

Common name: Ragged fringed-orchid.

Abundance: Occasional in the Anoka Sandplain, infrequent elsewhere.

Habitat: Acidic meadows, swales, swamps, thickets, and coniferous swamps. Usually found in full or partial sunlight, but sometimes in shade. Soil types range from sand to humic peat.

Known flowering dates: July 1-July 26.

Description: Stem 20-77 cm long (including inflorescence), glabrous; roots thick and fleshy; leaves 3 to 7 per stem, the lower ones lanceolate to elliptical, 5-14 cm long and 1.0-3.5 cm wide, the upper ones greatly

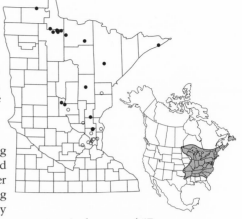

reduced in size, becoming bractlike; inflorescence a terminal raceme, 4-17 cm long, 2.0-4.5 cm wide, consisting of 15 to 60 white or greenish white flowers; floral bracts 0.7-2.2 cm long; ovaries 1.1-1.7 cm long, 1.0-2.8 mm wide at anthesis; sepals ovate to suborbicular, the lateral ones 3.0-7.0 mm long and 2.3-3.5 mm wide, the dorsal one similar but somewhat smaller; petals linear-oblong, 2.8-6.0 mm long, 0.7-1.3 mm wide; lip 0.5-1.9 cm wide, divided into three major segments, the lateral segments incised more than halfway to the base, producing a deep fringe of threadlike divisions, the medial segment incised less deeply or merely toothed; spur curved, 1.1-1.7 cm long.

Aid to identification: Although somewhat suggestive of a small *P. praeclara*, floral morphology indicates that the two species are only distantly related. In fact, they can be easily distinguished by the size of the flowers and especially the length of the spur (less than 2 cm long in *P. lacera*, more than 2 cm long in *P. praeclara*).

P. lacera is known to hybridize with the closely related *P. psycodes* to produce *P. Xandrewsii* M. White, which has whitish or rose-colored flowers and lips with fringes that are intermediate in length between the two parents. There are also reports of backcrosses that show a wider range of flower color and lip morphology (Case, 1987). No hybrids have been found in Minnesota yet, but they could turn up wherever the parents occur in close proximity.

Comments: The whitish flowers are fragrant in the evening, and are well adapted for pollination by crepuscular moths. For the human seeker this can be a surprisingly difficult plant to find in the thickets and swamps where it lives. It seems to be encountered most frequently in various low, wet habitats on the Anoka Sandplain, but populations are somewhat ephemeral.

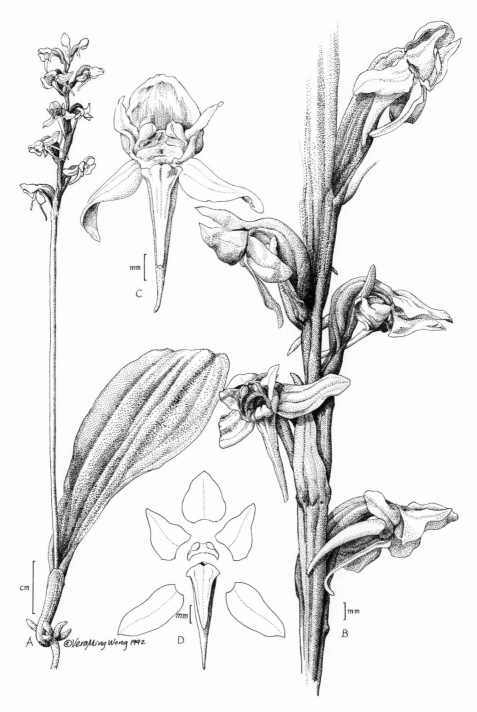

Platanthera obtusata **A**–Flowering plant, **B**–Inflorescence, **C**–Flower, **D**–
Flower, exploded view

Platanthera obtusata (Banks ex Pursh) Lindl.

Synonym: *Habenaria obtusata* (Banks ex Pursh) Rich.

Common name: Small northern bog-orchid.

Abundance: Relatively common.

Habitat: Most often in *Sphagnum*/coniferous swamps, typically in the shade of white cedar (*Thuja occidentalis*), black spruce (*Picea mariana*), or balsam fir (*Abies balsamea*). Less often in alder thickets and hardwood swamps.

Known flowering dates: June 17-August 5.

Description: Stem 8-28 cm long (including inflorescence), glabrous; roots fleshy; leaf one per stem, basal, obovate, 4.0-15.0 cm long, 1.5-4.4 cm wide; cauline bracts gener-

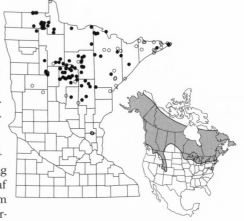

ally absent or occasionally with one present; inflorescence a terminal raceme, 2.0-11.0 cm long, 1.0-2.0 cm wide, consisting of 4 to 18 greenish flowers; floral bracts 0.4-1.7 cm long; ovaries 6.0-8.5 mm long, 1.0-1.8 mm wide at anthesis; dorsal sepal broadly ovate-orbicular, 2.0-4.0 mm long, 2.0-3.8 mm wide; lateral sepals ovate-lanceolate, 2.7-5.0 mm long, 1.4-2.2 mm wide at the widest point; petals lanceolate, dilated below the middle, 2.2-4.2 mm long, 0.7-1.2 mm wide; lip narrowly lanceolate, more or less dilated at base, 3.5-6.0 mm long, 0.3-0.8 mm wide near the middle; spur 4.5-7.0 mm long, curved, tapering to a pointed tip.

Aid to identification: The only species that could easily be confused with *P. obtusata* is the rare *P. clavellata*. Both are rather small, greenish swamp orchids with a single leaf. In *P. obtusata* the leaf is essentially basal, but in *P. clavellata* the leaf is attached some distance above the base. In swamp habitats the actual base may be below the surface of the living *Sphagnum*, making it necessary to excavate gently around the plant to discover where the leaf is attached.

Comments: This is the smallest and least conspicuous of the *Platanthera*s, but in northern Minnesota it is one of the most common. In ideal habitat (usually cedar swamps), it can become very abundant, sometimes with a hundred or more individuals occurring within a few square meters.

This is also perhaps the widest ranging of all our *Platanthera*s. It occurs across boreal North America, extending south into temperate regions and north into true arctic habitats. A smaller version (*P. obtusata* subsp. *oligantha* (Turcz.) Hulten) occurs in northern Europe and Asia.

It is known to be pollinated by female mosquitoes of the genus *Aedes* (Stoutamire, 1968), the same insects that pester humans, and by a small moth, *Anageshna primordialis* (Dyar) (Voss and Riefner, 1983).

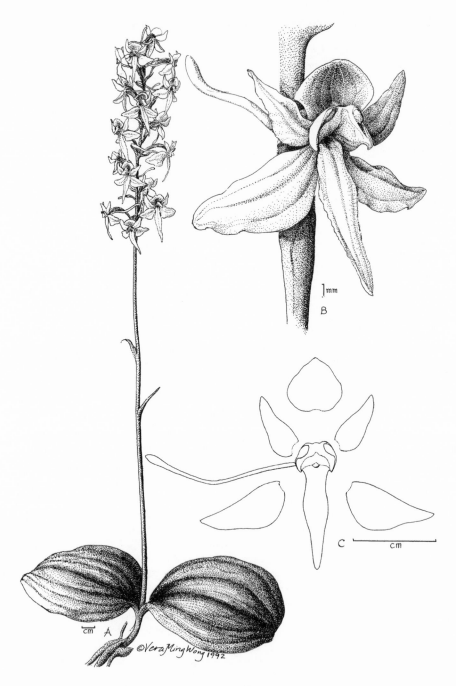

Platanthera orbiculata **A**–Flowering plant, **B**–Flower, **C**–Flower, exploded view

Platanthera orbiculata (Pursh) Lindl.

Synonym: *Habenaria orbiculata* (Pursh) Torr.

Common name: Large round-leaved orchid.

Abundance: Infrequent to occasional.

Habitat: Typically found in *Sphagnum/* coniferous swamps, in the shade of white cedar (*Thuja occidentalis*), black spruce (*Picea mariana*), or tamarack (*Larix laricina*). Occasionally seen in upland pine forests.

Known flowering dates: July 9-August 10.

Description: Stem 20-59 cm long (including inflorescence), glabrous; roots fleshy; leaves two per stem, opposite, basal, broadly elliptical to orbicular, 6-15 cm long, 3-15 cm

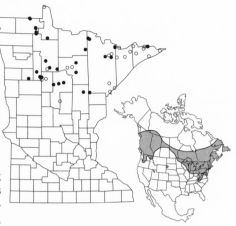

wide, widely spreading and more or less lying flat on the ground; cauline bracts 1 to 6, scattered below the inflorescence; inflorescence a terminal raceme, 6-21 cm long, 3-6 cm wide, consisting of 6 to 33 greenish white flowers (becoming light brown or straw-colored when dried); floral bracts 0.6-1.6 cm long; ovaries 0.9-1.5 cm long, 1.8-2.2 mm wide at anthesis, on apparent pedicels 4.0-10.0 mm long; dorsal sepal orbicular to depressed-orbicular, free from the petals, 3.5-6.0 mm long, 4.2-6.5 mm wide; lateral sepals irregularly ovate, 7.0-10.0 mm long, 4.0-5.3 mm wide at the widest point; petals narrowly ovate, 5.5-7.2 mm long, 2.2-3.0 mm wide at the widest point; lip entire, linear, with a blunt or rounded tip, 9-15 mm long and about 2 mm wide at the middle; spur 2.0-2.7 cm long, slightly thickened near the tip.

Aid to identification: Sometimes confused with *P. hookeri*, but reliably distinguished by a few simple characters. *P. orbiculata* will always have one or more bracts on the stem between the leaves and the inflorescence. These can be seen in the spring even before the inflorescence has developed and in the fall after the stem has become senescent. In addition, the lip has a distinctly club-shaped spur that is thicker at the tip than at the middle. In contrast, *P. hookeri* does not have any bracts on the stem, and the spur is narrower at the tip than at the middle.

Comments: An elegant species noted for its large shiny leaves, tall stem, and elusive nature. Although not as rare as sometimes thought, it is infrequently seen in any great numbers and usually occurs as scattered individuals or small colonies.

Stoutamire (1971) has reported two small gray moths (*Autographa ampla* and *Plusia balluca*) as pollinators.

Platanthera praeclara **A**–Flowering plant, **B**–Inflorescence, **C**–Flower, **D**–Flower, exploded view

Platanthera praeclara Sheviak & Bowles

Synonym: *Habenaria leucophaea* (Nutt.) A. Gray var. *praeclara* (Sheviak & Bowles) Cronq.

Common name: Western prairie fringed-orchid.

Abundance: Very rare. Federally threatened and state endangered. Report all sightings to the Minnesota DNR or the U.S. Fish and Wildlife Service.

Habitat: Calcareous meadows and prairies. Typically in low moist spots, but sometimes in well-drained soil; always in full sunlight.

Known flowering dates: July 1-July 29.

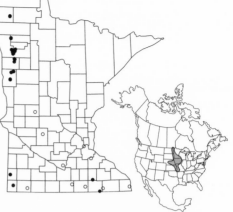

Description: Stems one or rarely two, 40-88 cm long (as short as 14 cm in drought-affected specimens), glabrous; roots thick and fleshy; leaves 5 to 10 per stem, the lower ones lanceolate to ovate-lanceolate, the bases strongly sheathing the stem, 9-15 cm long and 1.5-3.5 cm wide, the upper ones much reduced in size, becoming bractlike; inflorescence a terminal raceme, 5-15 cm long, 5-9 cm wide, consisting of 4 to 33 (usually fewer than 20) white flowers; floral bracts 2.0-6.5 cm long; ovaries 2.0-3.5 cm long, 1.6-2.2 mm wide at anthesis; sepals ovate to suborbicular, the lateral ones obliquely asymmetrical, 9-14 mm long, 6-9 mm wide; petals fan-shaped (flabelliform) with the apical margin shallowly and irregularly toothed, 1.0-1.7 cm long, 0.6-1.2 cm wide; lip 2.0-3.8 cm wide, divided into three major fan-shaped segments, the lateral segments incised more than half of the way to the base, producing a deep fringe, the medial segment usually incised less deeply; spur curved, 2.5-6.0 cm long.

Aid to identification: *P. praeclara* is most closely related to *P. psycodes* but is likely to be confused with *P. lacera*, the only other fringed-orchid in Minnesota with white flowers. *P. praeclara* is a much larger plant in all respects, particularly in the size of the flower and the length of the spur (see dichotomy 3 of the *Platanthera* key).

Until recently, *P. praeclara* was not recognized as distinct from the more easterly *P. leucophaea*, but now it is generally accepted that the two are distinct pollinator-isolated species (Sheviak and Bowles, 1986).

Comments: With the possible exception of the showy lady's-slipper (*Cypripedium reginae*), this is our largest and most spectacular orchid. Unfortunately, it is also our most threatened orchid. Over 95 percent of its prairie habitat has now been converted to farmland. As a result, its preservation as a species is a matter of immediate concern.

Its extremely long spur is intriguing, and apparently only the sphinx moths (*Sphingidae*) have a proboscis long enough to reach the nectar at its bottom (Sheviak and Bowles, 1986).

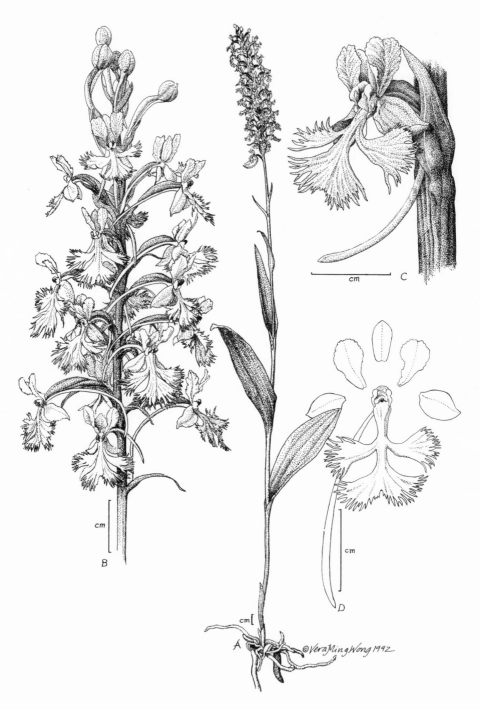

Platanthera psycodes **A**–Flowering plant, **B**–Inflorescence, **C**–Flower, **D**–Flower, exploded view

Platanthera psycodes (L.) Lindl.

Synonym: *Habenaria psycodes* (L.) Spreng.

Common name: Small purple fringed-orchid.

Abundance: Occasional to common.

Habitat: Swamp forests, wet woods, lake shores, stream banks, meadows, and shrub thickets. Most often in shallow organic or loamy soil, but also in silty, gravelly, or even rocky substrata; in shade or full sunlight.

Known flowering dates: July 8-August 22.

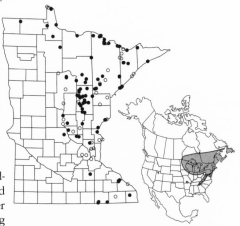

Description: Stem 44-100 cm long (including inflorescence), glabrous; roots thick and fleshy; leaves 4 to 12 per stem, the lower and medial ones elliptical, 10-17 cm long and 2.0-7.0 cm wide, the upper ones much reduced in size, becoming bract-like; inflorescence a terminal raceme, 4-22 cm long, 3.0-5.0 cm wide, consisting of 20-125 purplish flowers; floral bracts lance-linear, 1.0-3.5 cm long; ovaries 1.1-1.7 cm long, 0.8-2.4 mm wide at anthesis; sepals ovate to broadly elliptical or oblong, 4.0-6.5 mm long, 2.0-3.6 mm wide; petals obovate to spatulate, with shallowly and irregularly toothed margins (especially at apex), 4.0-8.0 mm long, 2.0-4.0 mm wide; lip 7.5-14.0 mm wide, divided into three major fan-shaped (flabelliform) segments, each segment incised less than half of the way to the base, resulting in a relatively shallow fringe; spur curved, 1.7-2.3 cm long.

Aid to identification: This is our only fringed-orchid that has purple flowers. It is closely related to the more easterly *P. grandiflora*, which for all appearances is a large-flowered version of our plant. There are, however, subtle morphological differences that result in reproductive isolation (Stoutamire, 1974). Although some of our more robust specimens do approach *P. grandiflora* in size of the flowers and inflorescence, they appear to be environmentally induced extremes of *P. psycodes*.

    P. psycodes is known to hybridize with *P. lacera* to produce *P.* X*andrewsii* M. White. Such hybrids reportedly have flower color and morphology intermediate between the parents. No such hybrids have yet been found in Minnesota, but pure white *P. psycodes* (f. *albiflora* (Bigel.) R. Hoffm.) have been found.

Comments: This is one of our most conspicuous orchids and is often seen along roadsides, especially where roads cut through wetlands. The state parks in the St. Croix Valley are good places to view this species, particularly the marshy terraces above the floodplain.

    It is reportedly visited by butterflies during the day and moths at night (Stoutamire, 1974).

The Genus Pogonia *Juss.*

The name *Pogonia* is from the Greek word meaning bearded, in reference to the bristles on the upper surface of the lip.

A small genus of fewer than 10 species, only one of which occurs in North America.

Pogonia ophioglossoides **A**–Flowering plant, **B**–Flower, **C**–Flower, exploded view

Pogonia ophioglossoides (L.) Juss.

Common name: Rose pogonia.

Abundance: Occasional to frequent.

Habitat: In strongly to weakly acidic peat-land habitats, particularly in *Sphagnum/* coniferous swamps and bogs, under a partial canopy of cedar (*Thuja*), spruce (*Picea*), or tamarack (*Larix*). Also in sedge meadows and floating mats.

Known flowering dates: June 14-July 30.

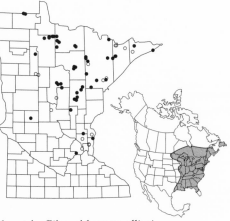

Description: Stem 15-45 cm long, slender, glabrous; lateral offshoots (stolons) giving rise to aerial shoots at intervals of 10 cm or more; leaf usually solitary, from about midway on the stem, elliptical, sessile, veiny, 3.0-12.0 cm long, 0.6-2.1 cm wide; flowers usually one per stem, pink to purple; floral bract leaflike, oblong to elliptical, 1.2-5.0 cm long, 2.0-10.0 mm wide; ovary slender, 1.2-1.8 cm long, 1.8-3.0 mm wide at anthesis; sepals elliptical, 1.3-2.4 cm long, 2.0-6.0 mm wide, widely spreading; petals broadly elliptical, 1.3-2.3 cm long, 0.7-1.2 cm wide, lip pinkish with purple veins, narrowly oblong-spatulate, widest near the apex, and more or less tapering to the base, 1.4-2.1 cm long, 5-10 mm wide at the widest point, conspicuously bearded with a crest of short fleshy bristles rising vertically from the upper portion of the lip, apical margin fringed; column 8-11 mm long.

Aid to identification: *P. ophioglossoides* shares several distinguishing features with *Arethusa bulbosa* and *Calopogon tuberosus*. All three have showy pink to purple flowers with a crest of fleshy yellow bristles on the lip. They also have inconspicuous leaves and occur in similar habitats. Not surprisingly, they all belong to the same tribe (*Epidendreae*), but otherwise are not closely related. Their similarities are thought to be an example of convergent evolution (Thien and Marcks, 1972). *P. ophioglossoides* is the only one of the three that has both a single flower and a single elliptical leaf that is attached near the middle of the stem.

A rare white-flowered form (f. *albiflora* Rand & Redfield) is known, and could be found as scattered individuals in a colony of normal-colored plants.

Comments: Still a fairly common plant in northeastern and north central Minnesota, but in recent years it has become increasingly rare in the Twin Cities area.

P. ophioglossoides is reportedly pollinated by bumblebees, which are initially attracted by the appearance of the large pink flower and by the floral fragrance. As the bee approaches the flower it is enticed by an ultraviolet signal to land on the lip. It then crawls down into the flower, seeking nectar, but finds little and attempts to leave. When backing out the bee picks up pollinia from the anther and deposits pollinia on the stigma (Thien and Marcks, 1972).

The Genus Spiranthes *Rich.*
(Ladies'-tresses orchids)
❧

The name *Spiranthes* is from the Greek words meaning "coiled flowers," in apparent reference to the spiraled arrangement of the flowers.

A highly technical and complex genus with worldwide distribution. As many as 300 species have been described, with about 20 in North America and four in Minnesota.

Correctly identifying specimens of *Spiranthes* can be very difficult and sometimes frustrating. Considerable patience is required to recognize the fine distinctions that separate some of the species. For this reason it is highly recommended that living specimens be studied whenever possible. If only dried specimens are available, the flowers can frequently be restored to a lifelike appearance by soaking them in hot water.

A Key to the *Spiranthes* of Minnesota

1. Perianth 3.5–6.2 mm long; leaves ovate-elliptical, 1.8–5.0 cm long; inflorescence consisting of flowers in a single rank (vertical column).

S. lacera

1. Perianth 6.5–12.0 mm long; leaves linear (or absent at flowering time), 5.0–28 cm long; inflorescence consisting of flowers in two or more ranks.

   2. Lateral sepals connivent with the dorsal sepal and petals forming a "hood" that more or less arches over the column; lip strongly constricted near the middle, appearing fiddle-shaped (pandurate) when viewed from above.

   S. romanzoffiana

   2. Lateral sepals separate from the dorsal sepal and petals, not forming an obvious hood; lip not constricted, or only slightly constricted near the middle, not fiddle-shaped.

      3. Leaves present at flowering time; lip constricted slightly near the middle; middle and upper bracts not generally overlapping; lateral sepals more or less appressed.

      S. cernua

      3. Leaves absent at flowering time; lip not constricted; middle and upper bracts generally overlapping; lateral sepals curved and spreading, often arching over the top of the flower (not always apparent in pressed specimens).

      S. magnicamporum

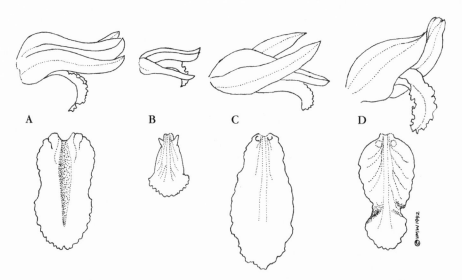

Figure 8. Flowers and lips of *Spiranthes: A—S. cernua, B—S. lacera, C—S. magnicamporum, D—S. romanzoffiana* (all shown approximately 3.5X actual size)

*Many orchids find refuge in the pine forests
scattered throughout northern Minnesota.*

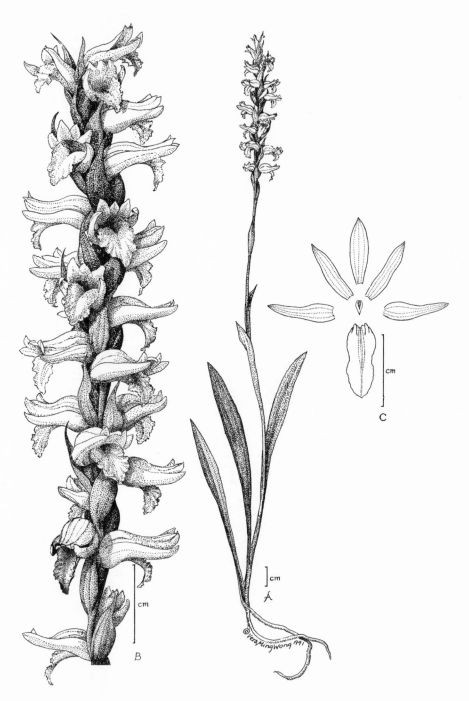

Spiranthes cernua **A**–Flowering plant, **B**–Inflorescence, **C**–Flower, exploded view

Spiranthes cernua (L.) Rich.

Common name: Nodding ladies'-tresses.

Abundance: Occasional, but spotty and somewhat ephemeral.

Habitat: Meadows and lakeshores; apparently preferring acidic or circumneutral substrata. Usually found in short or sparse vegetation where competition is minimal; also in areas of local disturbance, where it functions as an effective colonizer.

Known flowering dates: July 21-September 19.

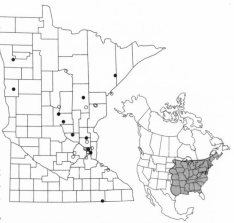

Description: Stem 10-40 cm long (including inflorescence), pubescent above; roots relatively thick and fleshy; leaves essentially basal, generally present at flowering time, linear to narrowly oblanceolate, 6-28 cm long, 0.4-1.4 cm wide; cauline bracts 3 to 5, the upper ones not generally overlapping (the tip of one bract not quite reaching the base of the bract above); inflorescence 2.5-11.0 cm long, consisting of 9 to 35 white flowers densely packed in two or more ranks (vertical columns), more or less spirally twisted on the stem; floral bracts ovate-acuminate, 7-17 mm long; ovaries essentially sessile, 3.3-6.5 mm long, 1.6-3.7 mm wide; perianth 8.0-12.0 mm long; sepals more or less appressed, lanceolate, 5.5-11.0 mm long, 1.2-2.2 mm wide at widest point; petals similar to sepals; lip ovate to oblong, slightly constricted near the middle, the portion above the constriction recurved and with a ragged, wavy margin, 5.5-11.0 mm long, 3.0-6.0 mm wide; calli (two hard protuberances) at base of lip prominent, longer than wide, often 1 mm long or longer.

Aid to identification: Very similar to *S. magnicamporum*, and until recently they were both considered members of the same polymorphic species (Sheviak, 1973). The easiest way to tell them apart is by the basal leaves. In *S. cernua* the leaves are present at flowering time, but in *S. magnicamporum* they wither at least two weeks before the flowers appear.

   S. cernua is reported to hybridize with *S. lacera* and *S. romanzoffiana* (the latter named *S.* X*steigeri* Correll). Hybrids with *S. magnicamporum* would also seem likely.

Comments: Individual colonies seem to be somewhat transient; they rapidly colonize newly created habitats but thrive only in the early stages of succession. This is an effective strategy, and is abetted by an accelerated life cycle. Seeds mature rapidly, and new plants can apparently reach reproductive size in only two years (Stoutamire, 1964).

   Reports of *S. cernua* occurring along our northern border (Lakela, 1965; Ownbey and Morley, 1991) are based on misidentified specimens of *S. romanzoffiana*. Apparently *S. cernua* is rare or absent in northern boreal-type habitats.

   Reported to be pollinated by bumblebees (Catling, 1983b).

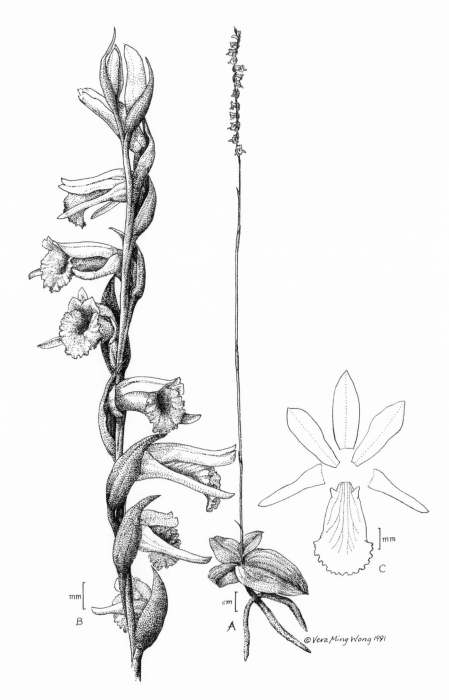

Spiranthes lacera **A**–Flowering plant, **B**–Portion of inflorescence, **C**–Flower, exploded view

Spiranthes lacera (Raf.) Raf.

Synonym: *Spiranthes gracilis* (Bigel.) Beck.

Common name: Northern slender ladies'-tresses.

Abundance: Occasional to locally frequent.

Habitat: Most of the records are from upland coniferous forests, especially sandy pine forests (including plantations). It also occurs, but less often, in swamp forests and on river banks, rocky barrens, and cliffs.

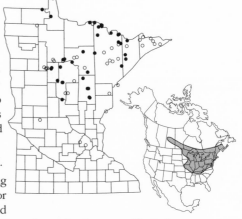

Known flowering dates: July 11-August 21.

Description: Stem to 45 cm long (including inflorescence), essentially glabrous or sparsely pubescent above; roots thick and fleshy; leaves basal, somewhat faded or withered at anthesis; ovate-elliptical, usually with a short but distinct petiole, veiny, 1.8-5.0 cm long, 0.7-2.0 cm wide; cauline bracts 4 to 6; inflorescence 2.5-15.0 cm long, consisting of 7 to 45 white flowers loosely arranged in a single rank (vertical column), spirally twisted on the stem or occasionally secund; floral bracts ovate-acuminate, 3.5-8.5 mm long; ovaries essentially sessile, 2.0-5.5 mm long, 1.3-2.0 mm wide; perianth 3.5-6.2 mm long; sepals lanceolate to linear, 3.5-6.2 mm long, 0.3-1.0 mm wide; petals similar to sepals; lip oblong, with a ragged wavy margin on the apical portion, 4.0-6.0 mm long, 1.5-2.8 mm wide; calli (two hard protuberances) at base of lip small, erect.

Aid to identification: This is a delicate plant easily distinguished from the other *Spiranthes* by its single column of small flowers (the perianth rarely exceeds 6 mm in length) and by its ovate leaves. The sterile rosettes are often seen in the spring and look very much like *Goodyera repens* var. *ophioides*. But *S. lacera* usually occurs in upland forests, and *G. repens* var. *ophioides* usually occurs in bogs and swamps. Also, *S. lacera* has thick fleshy roots that look like vertical tuberoids, whereas *G. repens* var. *ophioides* has a branched horizontal rhizome. When the flowering stalk appears in July, identification is easily determined by comparing floral morphology (see dichotomy 14 of the key to Minnesota orchids at the beginning of this book).

There are reports of hybridization with *S. cernua*, *S. magnicamporum*, and *S. romanzoffiana* (Simpson and Catling, 1978), but to date only suspected hybrids with *S. romanzoffiana* have been found in Minnesota. These specimens (from St. Louis County) have floral and leaf morphology intermediate between the putative parents, but the flowers are arranged in a single rank like *S. lacera*.

Comments: This is probably the most common *Spiranthes* in Minnesota, and it seems to have the potential to be found throughout much of the forested region of the state, even in the southeastern counties.

Reported to be pollinated by bumblebees (Catling, 1983b) and by several genera and species of small bees (Luer, 1975).

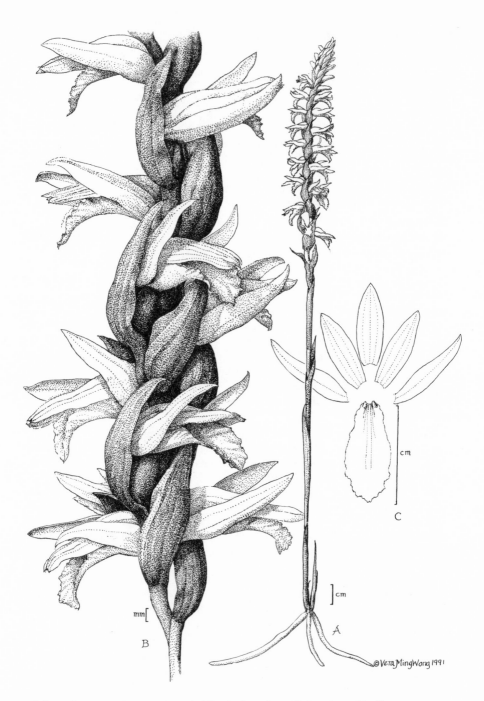

Spiranthes magnicamporum ***A***–Flowering plant, ***B***–Portion of inflorescence,
C–Flower, exploded view

Spiranthes magnicamporum Sheviak

Common name: Great Plains ladies'-tresses.

Abundance: Occasional.

Habitat: Meadows, prairies, and grassy openings. Typically in low moist spots, but also in dry, gravelly bluff prairies on the Paleozoic Plateau in the southeastern counties. It apparently prefers circumneutral or calcareous soils.

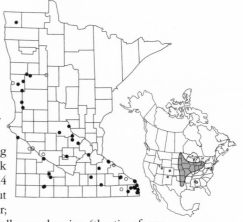

Known flowering dates: August 27-September 24.

Description: Stem 15-42 cm long (including inflorescence), pubescent above; roots thick and fleshy; leaves essentially basal, up to 14 cm long and 1.2 cm wide, withering about two weeks before the flowers appear; cauline bracts 4 to 6, the upper ones usually overlapping (the tip of one bract reaching the base of the bract above); inflorescence 2.5-10.0 cm long, consisting of 13 to 48 white flowers densely packed in two or more ranks (vertical columns), gently spiraled on the stem or nearly vertical; floral bracts ovate-acuminate, 7-23 mm long; ovaries sessile, 4.3-8.0 mm long, 1.2-3.1 mm wide; perianth 8.0-12.0 mm long; lateral sepals curved and spreading, often arching above the flower (not always apparent in pressed specimens), lanceolate, 7.0-11.0 mm long, 1.5-2.5 mm wide at widest point; petals similar to sepals; lip oblong-ovate, not constricted near the middle, appearing to taper or curve evenly from the base to the tip, the upper portion with a ragged wavy margin, 7.0-11.0 mm long, 3.5-6.0 mm wide; calli (two hard protuberances) at the base of the lip not prominent, usually less than 1 mm long.

Aid to identification: *S. magnicamporum* has only recently been recognized as distinct from *S. cernua* (Sheviak, 1973), and although the two species are very similar they can be told apart with a little practice. The absence of basal leaves at flowering time is the easiest method, and is reliable more than 90 percent of the time. Floral morphology is also diagnostic, but subtle; if collecting specimens, the position of the lateral sepals and the shape of the lip should be noted and compared to the illustrations before pressing.

It has been reported to hybridize with *S. lacera*, and can be expected to hybridize with *S. cernua.*

Comments: Most people still fail to distinguish this species from *S. cernua,* and as a result we have relatively little data, or even reliable observations, concerning its natural history. The collection record does indicate that it is more common than *S. cernua* and occurs in similar habitats, except for its unexpected occurrence on dry bluff prairies in the southeast. It also seems to flower later in the year, which may impart some degree of reproductive isolation.

Spiranthes romanzoffiana **A**–Flowering plant, **B**–Inflorescence, **C**–Flower, exploded view

Spiranthes romanzoffiana Cham.

Common name: Hooded ladies'-tresses.

Abundance: Locally frequent in the northwest, occasional elsewhere.

Habitat: It occurs most often in fens, meadows, and open coniferous swamps; these are typically *Sphagnum* or sedge-dominated habitats. It occurs less often on sandy beaches and gravelly or rocky lakeshores.

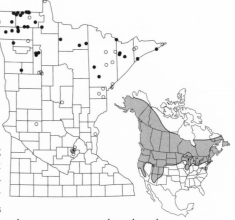

Known flowering dates: July 17-August 28.

Description: Stem 13-46 cm long (including inflorescence), more or less pubescent above; roots thick and fleshy; leaves present at flowering time, linear to narrowly lanceolate or oblanceolate, the lower ones 5-24 cm long, 2.5-9.0 mm wide, the middle and upper ones much reduced, becoming essentially bracts; inflorescence 2.5-13.0 cm long, consisting of 11 to 45 white flowers in two or more ranks (vertical columns), more or less spirally twisted on the stem; floral bracts ovate-acuminate, 8-20 mm long; ovaries essentially sessile, 3.5-5.5 mm long, 1.3-2.5 mm wide; perianth 6.5-11.5 mm long; sepals and petals connivent to form a "hood" that more or less arches over the lip; lip strongly constricted above the middle, producing a fiddle-shaped (pandurate) appearance when flattened and viewed from above (not easily seen in herbarium specimens), the portion above the constriction with a ragged wavy margin, or nearly entire, 6.0-11.5 mm long, 3.0-4.5 mm wide at its widest point; calli (two hard protuberances) at base of lip small.

Aid to identification: It is often mistaken for *S. cernua* or *S. magnicamporum*, but once the distinctive "hood" is recognized, it becomes easy to separate this species from all look-alikes. In pressed specimens it is sometimes difficult to tell if the sepals and petals are actually united to form a hood, or are merely pressed together. Likewise, the fiddle-shaped lip is very distinctive but not easily recognized in pressed specimens.

Putative hybrids with *S. cernua* have been named *S.* X*steigeri* Correll, but none has been found in Minnesota yet. Probable hybrids with *S. lacera* have been found in northern St. Louis County. These specimens have floral and leaf morphology intermediate between the putative parents, and flowers are arranged in a single rank.

Comments: The habitat of this species includes some of the largest swamps and sedge meadows in northern Minnesota. Yet, even in a vast expanse of apparently ideal habitat, populations usually consist of only a few scattered individuals. The populations do not seem to experience the boom and bust cycles seen in other species of *Spiranthes.*

Reported to be pollinated by bumblebees (*Bombus* spp.) and smaller halictine bees (Catling, 1983b).

Appendix

Known flowering dates for Minnesota's orchids

Species name	May	June	July	Aug.	Sept.	Oct.
Amerorchis rotundifolia (small round-leaved orchis)		■	■			
Aplectrum hyemale (putty root)		■				
Arethusa bulbosa (dragon's-mouth)		■	■			
Calopogon tuberosus (grass-pink)			■			
Calypso bulbosa var. *americana* (fairy slipper)		■				
Coeloglossum viride var. *virescens* (long-bracted orchid)		■	■			
Corallorhiza maculata (spotted coral-root)			■			
Corallorhiza odontorhiza (autumn coral-root)				■	■	■
Corallorhiza striata (striped coral-root)		■				
Corallorhiza trifida (early coral-root)	■	■				
Cypripedium acaule (stemless lady's-slipper)		■				
Cypripedium arietinum (ram's-head lady's-slipper)	■	■				
Cypripedium calceolus var. *parviflorum* (small yellow lady's-slipper)	■	■				

Known flowering dates for Minnesota's orchids *(continued)*

Species name	May	June	July	Aug.	Sept.	Oct.
Cypripedium calceolus var. *pubescens* (large yellow lady's-slipper)	■	■				
Cypripedium candidum (small white lady's-slipper)	■	■				
Cypripedium reginae (showy lady's-slipper)		■				
Galearis spectabilis (showy orchis)	■					
Goodyera pubescens (downy rattlesnake plantain)				■		
Goodyera repens var. *ophioides* (lesser rattlesnake plantain)			■	■		
Goodyera tesselata (tesselated rattlesnake plantain)			■	■		
Liparis lilifolia (lily-leaved twayblade)		■				
Liparis loeselii (Loesel's twayblade)		■	■			
Listera auriculata (auricled twayblade)		■				
Listera convallarioides (broad-leaved twayblade)			?			
Listera cordata (heart-leaved twayblade)		■	■			
Malaxis monophyllos var. *brachypoda* (white adder's-mouth)		■	■			
Malaxis paludosa (bog adder's-mouth)			■	■		
Malaxis unifolia (green adder's-mouth)		■	■			
Platanthera clavellata (small green wood-orchid)			■			
Platanthera dilatata (tall white bog-orchid)			■			

Known flowering dates for Minnesota's orchids *(continued)*

Species name	May	June	July	Aug.	Sept.	Oct.
Platanthera flava var. *herbiola* (tubercled rein-orchid)			▓			
Platanthera hookeri (Hooker's orchid)		▓	▓			
Platanthera hyperborea (northern bog-orchid)		▓	▓	▓		
Platanthera lacera (ragged fringed-orchid)			▓			
Platanthera obtusata (small northern bog-orchid)		▓	▓	▓		
Platanthera orbiculata (large round-leaved orchid)			▓	▓		
Platanthera praeclara (western prairie fringed-orchid)			▓			
Platanthera psycodes (small purple fringed-orchid)			▓	▓		
Pogonia ophioglossoides (rose pogonia)		▓	▓			
Spiranthes cernua (nodding ladies'-tresses)				▓	▓	
Spiranthes lacera (northern slender ladies'-tresses)			▓	▓		
Spiranthes magnicamporum (Great Plains ladies'-tresses)					▓	
Spiranthes romanzoffiana (hooded ladies'-tresses)				▓		

Glossary

🌿

Acuminate Tapering to a slender point.

Acute Ending in a point that forms an angle measuring less than 90°.

Albino An abnormal absence of pigmentation. Used more often in reference to animals than to plants.

Alluvial Pertaining to sediments deposited by a river.

Anther The portion of the stamen that contains the pollen.

Anthesis The expansion or the time of expansion of a flower.

Apex The uppermost point.

Apiculate Having a short sharp point, as at the tip of a leaf.

Appressed Pressed close to or lying flat against something.

Auricle A small lobe or "ear," often as an appendage at the base of a leaf or in the case of orchids at the base of a floral lip.

Basal Relating to or situated at the base of something, as in leaves occurring at the base of a stem.

Beak A pointed projection.

Blade The expanded portion of a leaf.

Bog Narrowly defined by ecologists as a wetland on deep peat isolated from groundwater, and with a pH less than 4.6. Characteristically with a ground cover of *Sphagnum* moss and an overstory (when present) of black spruce (*Picea mariana*) and lesser amounts of tamarack (*Larix laricina*). In common usage the term describes any plant community or habitat on saturated acidic peat.

Boreal Relating to northern regions. In the case of plant habitats it usually refers to the area between the arctic region and the temperate region. There is much dispute among ecologists as to whether true boreal conditions exist in Minnesota.

Bract A structure closely resembling a leaf (and evolutionarily derived from a leaf) but greatly reduced in size, especially the blade. Referred to as a cauline bract when located between the inflorescence and the leaves, and as a floral bract when subtending a flower.

Bulbous Resembling a bulb.

Calcareous Usually applied to water or soil that contains calcium or calcium carbonate, and as a result has a pH greater than 7.

Capitate Shaped like a head, or having a head; abruptly enlarged.

Capsule A term describing the ovary once it has become mature and dry; essentially, the object containing the ripened seeds.

Cauline Belonging to the stem, or arising from it.

Ciliate Fringed with small hairs (cilia).

Circumneutral Referring to a pH value of approximately 7.0.

Clavate Shaped like a club; gradually thickened near the distal end.

Column A floral structure unique to orchids composed of the fused style and filaments.

Congeneric Referring to two or more species that belong to the same genus.

Conifer A cone-bearing tree belonging to the order Coniferales; in Minnesota that includes pine (*Pinus* spp.), fir (*Abies balsamea*), spruce (*Picea* spp.), tamarack (*Larix laricina*), cedar (*Thuja occidentalis*), and juniper (*Juniperus* spp.).

Coniferous swamp A swamp dominated by coniferous tree species, typically white cedar (*Thuja occidentalis*) with lesser amounts of tamarack (*Larix laricina*) and black spruce (*Picea mariana*).

Connivent Coming into contact or converging.

Coralloid Having the appearance and texture of coral.

Cordate Shaped like a heart, with the broader end at the base.

Corm A thickened underground stem.

Crenulate A minutely scalloped margin.

Cuneate Wedge-shaped; narrowly triangular with the acute angle toward the base.

Cylindrical Shaped like a cylinder.

Dilated Expanded laterally.

Dorsal Located on the back or top; specifically, the upperside of a flower or leaf.

Elliptical A narrow oval, tapering evenly at both ends like a football (in outline).

Endemic Confined to a specific region.

Entire Having a continuous, smooth margin; not toothed, notched, or fringed.

Erose Having an uneven or irregularly notched margin.

Falcate Hooked or curved like a sickle.

Fen A sedge-dominated wetland on deep or shallow peat with groundwater influence, and with a pH greater than 4.6.

Fibrous Being slender, threadlike, or stringlike, usually applied to structures such as roots.

Filiform Shaped like a filament; threadlike.

Flabelliform Shaped like a fan.

Floating mat A mat of vegetation or peat floating on the surface of water, usually at the margin of a small lake or slow-moving stream.

Foliaceous Resembling foliage, i.e., a leaf.

Form (*forma*) A taxonomic category with a hierarchical rank below that of a variety. Usually used to describe minor color variation.

Genus A taxonomic category with a hierarchical rank between that of species and family.

Glabrous Smooth, without hairs.

Glandular Bearing glands (secreting structures on the surface of the plant).

Globular Having the shape of a globe; spherical.

Habitat The place, or type of place, where a species or community lives; usually described in terms of geography, vegetation, climate, geology, and so on.

Hardwood swamp A swamp dominated by hardwood tree species, typically black ash (*Fraxinus nigra*) with lesser amounts of yellow birch (*Betula alleghaniensis*) and American elm (*Ulmus americanus*).

Inflorescence The flowering part of the plant.

Lanceolate Shaped like the head of a lance; tapering from the base to the apex, many times longer than wide.

Linear Long and narrow with parallel sides.

Lip One of the three petals in an orchid flower. Usually larger than and different in shape from the other two. In a normal resupinate flower it is the lowermost of the perianth parts.

Lobe A segment or division of an organ, like a rounded protuberance on the margin of a floral lip.

Marsh An emergent wetland characteristically dominated by cattail (*Typha* spp.) and/or bulrush (*Scirpus* spp.) on mineral soil in shallow stagnant water.

Meadow A vague term historically applied to various grass-, sedge-, or forb-dominated wetlands, usually with saturated soil but without standing water.

Mesic Moderately moist.

Monotypic A taxonomic category that contains only one representative, like a genus that contains only one species.

Morphological Relating to form or structure.

Oblanceolate Inverted lanceolate.

Oblong Resembling an elongate oval but with nearly parallel sides, usually two or three times longer than wide.

Obovate Inverted ovate.

Obtuse A blunt or rounded end that forms an angle measuring greater than 90°.

Orbicular Circular.

Ovary The part of the flower that develops into the fruit.

Ovate Shaped like an egg (in outline), with the broader end basal.

Pandurate Shaped like a fiddle in outline.

Peat A soil type developed under saturated conditions and composed of partially decomposed plant material.

Peatland An area of land covered with peat.

Pedicel The stem or stalk of a single flower.

Peduncle The stem or stalk of a single flower or a cluster of flowers.

Perianth That part of the flower consisting of the petals and sepals.

Petaloid Like a petal in appearance.

Petiole The stem or stalk of a leaf.

pH A term used to express the degree of acidity and alkalinity. Measured on a scale of 0–14 with 7 being neutral; the larger the number the more alkaline or calcareous, the lower the number the more acidic. When applied to orchid habitats in Minnesota, pH values range from about 3.8 (bog) to about 8.3 (calcareous fen).

Phenology The study of the relationship between climate and periodic biological phenomena. For example, the timing of the appearance of flowers, the maturation of seeds, and so on.

Pollen Single-cell spores produced by the anther, resulting in fertilization when deposited on the stigma.

Pollinium (*pl.* **pollinia**) A coherent mass of pollen.

Polymorphic With several or various forms.

Pouch A floral structure modified into a pouchlike shape, as in the lip of *Cypripedium.*

Prairie A native plant community dominated by grasses.

Pseudobulb A thickened portion of the stem; bulblike.

Pubescent Having hairs; being covered in hairs.

Quadrate Being square or approximately square.

Raceme A simple inflorescence of pedicellate flowers arranged on a common, more or less elongated axis.

Resupinate The flower twisting approximately 180° so that the lip, which would otherwise be uppermost, becomes lowermost.

Reticulate Resembling a net.

Rhizome An underground stem giving rise to roots at its nodes and the aerial stem at its tip. Often rootlike in appearance.

Root The underground portion of the plant that absorbs moisture and nutrients. Morphologically and functionally distinct from rhizomes, bulbs, corms, and other underground structures that are modified portions of the stem, and therefore possess nodes and internodes.

Rosette A cluster of basal leaves arranged radially or spirally.

Saccate Having the shape of a sac or pouch.

Saprophyte A plant that derives its nourishment by decomposing dead organic matter.

Scape Essentially a peduncle arising from the ground. Differing from a stem in not bearing leaves or bracts.

Secund Having the flowers of an inflorescence all face to one side.

Sedge Any member of the sedge family (*Cyperaceae*), especially of the genus *Carex.*

Seep A term usually applied to a wetland sustained by a diffuse discharge of groundwater.

Senescent Old; having become dried or shriveled with age.

Sessile Without a stalk or stem; attached directly to the base.

Sheath As used here, the lower part of the leaf, which may form a tubular envelope around the stem or pseudobulb. Usually with an expanded blade, but sometimes without.

Shrub swamp A swamp dominated by shrubs, typically alder (*Alnus incana* subsp. *rugosa*), willow (*Salix* spp.), and dogwood (*Cornus* spp.).

Spatulate Shaped like a spatula; oblong, with the basal end narrowed.

Spike A simple inflorescence of sessile flowers arranged on a common axis.

Spur A hollow tubular structure projecting roughly downward or laterally from the base of the lip; usually containing nectar.

Stamen The male reproductive structure of the flower, consisting of the anther and filament.

Sterile When used in reference to orchids, it means a plant without fruit or flowers.

Stolon A runner or horizontal offshoot from the stem.

Subulate Awl-shaped; relatively long, narrow, and sharply pointed.

Swale A general habitat term applied to a variety of low, moist depressions.

Swamp A much-abused term narrowly defined here as a forested or shrub-dominated wetland on deep or shallow peat with some groundwater influence, and a pH greater than 4.6. Often (and incorrectly) used interchangeably with bog.

Taxon A taxonomic group or entity of any rank.

Temperate Used in the context of orchid habitats to describe a moderate climate, or a geographical region characterized by a moderate climate; the habitat zone directly south of the boreal zone.

Tepal A petal or a sepal.

Truncate Ending abruptly, as if cut off transversely.

Tubercle A small knobby prominence.

Tuberoid A thickened tuberlike root.

Undulate Having a wavy margin.

Variety A taxonomic category with a hierarchical rank below the level of subspecies.

Ventral Located on the bottom; specifically, the underside of a flower or leaf.

Literature Cited

❦

Ackerman, J. D., and M. R. Mesler. 1979. Pollination biology of *Listera cordata* (orchidaceae). American Journal of Botany 66:820-24.

Arditti, J., J. D. Michaud, and P. L. Healey. 1979. Morphometry of orchid seeds. I. Native California and related species of *Cypripedium*. American Journal of Botany 60:1129-39.

Atwood, J. T. 1986. The size of the Orchidaceae and the systematic distribution of ephiphytic orchids. Selbyana 9:171-86.

Auclair, A. N. 1972. Comparative ecology of the orchids *Aplectrum hyemale* and *Orchis spectabilis*. Bulletin of the Torrey Botanical Club 99:1-10.

Baldwin, J. T. 1970. White phase in flower development in *Cypripedium acaule*. Rhodora 72:142-43.

Baldwin, W. K. W. 1961. *Malaxis paludosa* (L.) sw. in the Hudson Bay lowlands. Canadian Field-Naturalist 75:74-77.

Boyden, T. C. 1982. The pollination biology of *Calypso bulbosa* var. *americana* (Orchidaceae): Initial deception of bumblebee visitors. Oecologia 55:178-84.

Brumback, W. E. 1990. Commercial production of terrestrial orchids—what's being done? *In*: Proceedings from a conference: North American native terrestrial orchid propagation and production. 84-86.

Campbell, E. O. 1970. Morphology of the fungal association in three species of *Corallorhiza* in Michigan. Michigan Botanist 9:108-13.

Case, F. W. 1987. *Orchids of the western Great Lakes region*. Cranbrook Institute of Science. 251 pp.

Catling, P. M. 1976. On the geographical distribution, ecology and distinctive features of *Listera X veltmanii* Case. Rhodora 78:261-69.

——. 1982. Breeding systems of northeastern North American *Spiranthes* (Orchidaceae). Canadian Journal of Botany 60:3017-39.

——. 1983a. Antogamy in eastern Canadian Orchidaceae: A review of current knowledge and some new observations. Le Naturaliste Canadian 110:37-53.

——. 1983b. Pollination of northeastern North American *Spiranthes* (Orchidaceae). Canadian Journal of Botany 61:1080-93.

——, and G. Knerer. 1980. Pollination of the small white lady's-slipper (*Cypripe-*

dium candidum) in Lambton County, Southern Ontario. Canadian Field-Naturalist 94:435-38.

Close, R. C., N. T. Moore, A. I. Tomlinson, and A. D. Low. 1978. Aerial dispersal of biological material from Australia to New Zealand. International Journal of Biometeorology 22:1-19.

Correll, D. S. 1978. *Native orchids of North America north of Mexico.* Stanford University Press, Stanford. 399 pp.

Curtis, J. T. 1939. The relation of specificity of orchid mycorrhizal fungi to the problem of symbiosis. American Journal of Botany 26:390-98.

———. 1943. Germination and seedling development in five species of *Cypripedium.* American Journal of Botany 30:199-206.

Dressler, R. L. 1981. *The orchids: Natural history and classification.* Harvard University Press, Cambridge. 332 pp.

Freudenstein, J. V. 1987. A preliminary study of *Corallorhiza maculata* (Orchidaceae) in eastern North America. Contributions from the University of Michigan Herbarium 16:145-53.

Gandawijaja, D., and J. Arditti. 1983. The orchids of Krakatau: Evidence for a mode of transport. Annals of Botany 52:127-30.

Hogan, K. P. 1983. The pollination biology and breeding system of *Aplectrum hyemale* (Orchidaceae). Canadian Journal of Botany 61:1906-10.

Kallunki, J. A. 1976. Population studies in *Goodyera* (Orchidaceae) with emphasis on the hybrid origin of *G. tesselata.* Brittonia 28:53-75.

———. 1981. Reproductive biology of mixed-species populations of *Goodyera* (Orchidaceae) in northern Michigan. Brittonia 33:137-55.

Klier, K., M. J. Leoschke, and J. F. Wendel. 1991. Hybridization and introgression in white and yellow ladyslipper orchids (*Cypripedium candidum* and *C. pubescens*). Journal of Heredity 82:305-18.

Lakela, O. 1951. Previously unreported plants from Minnesota. Rhodora 53:159-60.

———. 1965. *A flora of northeastern Minnesota.* University of Minnesota Press, Minneapolis. 541 pp.

Luer, C. A. 1975. *The native orchids of the United States and Canada excluding Florida.* The New York Botanical Garden, New York. 361 pp.

MacDougal, D. T. 1895. Poisonous influence of various species of *Cypripedium.* Bulletin of the Geological and Natural History Survey of Minnesota 9:450-51.

MacMillan, C. 1892. *The metaspermae of the Minnesota Valley.* Geological and Natural History Survey of Minnesota, Minneapolis. 826 pp.

Mosquin, T. 1970. The reproductive biology of *Calypso bulbosa* (Orchidaceae). Canadian Field-Naturalist 84:291-96.

Ownbey, G. B., and T. Morley. 1991. *Vascular plants of Minnesota: A checklist and atlas.* University of Minnesota Press, Minneapolis. 307 pp.

Reeves, L. M., and T. Reeves. 1984. Life history and reproduction of *Malaxis paludosa* in Minnesota. American Orchid Society Bulletin 53:1280-91.

Robinson, H., and P. Burns-Balogh. 1982. Evidence for a primatively epiphytic habit in Orchidaceae. Systematic Botany 7:353-58.

Sheviak, C. J. 1973. A new *Spiranthes* from the grasslands of central North America. Botanical Museum Leaflets, Harvard University 23:285-97.

——, and M. L. Bowles. 1986. The prairie fringed orchids: a pollinator-isolated species pair. Rhodora 88:267-90.

Simpson, R. C., and P. M. Catling. 1978. *Spiranthes lacera* X *S. romanzoffiana,* a new natural hybrid orchid from Ontario. Canadian Field-Naturalist 92:350-58.

Stoutamire, W. P. 1964. Seeds and seedlings of native orchids. Michigan Botanist 3:107-19.

——. 1967. Flower biology of the lady's-slippers. Michigan Botanist 6:159-75.

——. 1968. Mosquito pollination of *Habenaria obtusata* (Orchidaceae). Michigan Botanist 7:203-12.

——. 1971. Pollination in temperate American orchids. *In:* Proceedings of the 6th World Orchid Conference, ed. M. J. G. Corrigan, Halstead Press, Sydney. 233-43.

——. 1974. Relationships of the purple-fringed orchids *Platanthera psycodes* and *P. grandiflora.* Brittonia 26:42-58.

Stuckey, I. H. 1967. Environmental factors and the growth of native orchids. American Journal of Botany 54:232-41.

Summerhayes, V. S. 1951. *Wild orchids of Britain.* Collins, London. 345 pp.

Taylor, R. L. 1967. The foliar embryos of *Malaxis paludosa.* Canadian Journal of Botany 45:1553-56.

Thien, L. B., and B. G. Marcks. 1972. The floral biology of *Arethusa bulbosa, Calopogon tuberosus,* and *Pogonia ophioglossoides* (Orchidaceae). Canadian Journal of Botany 50:2319-25.

Van Der Pijl, L., and C. H. Dodson. 1966. *Orchid flowers: Their pollination and evolution.* University of Miami Press, Coral Gables. 214 pp.

Voss, E. G. 1966. Nomenclatural notes on monocots. Rhodora 68:435-63.

——, and R. E. Riefner. 1983. A pyralid moth (Lepidoptera) as pollinator of blunt-leaf orchis. The Great Lakes Entomologist 16:57-60.

Whiting, R. E., and P. M. Catling. 1986. *Orchids of Ontario.* The Canacoll Foundation, Ottawa. 169 pp.

Index

𝕉

Welby R. Smith has been the botanist of the Natural Heritage Program of the Minnesota Department of Natural Resources since the program's inception in 1979, and is also the coordinator of the endangered plant species program for the DNR. He was a contributor to *Minnesota's Endangered Flora and Fauna* (Minnesota, 1988).

Vera Ming Wong is a natural science illustrator and artist. Her drawings of plants, animals, and habitats have been published in several books and journals, including *Minnesota's Endangered Flora and Fauna* and *Northwoods Wildlife: A Watcher's Guide to Habitats.* She is a member of the Guild of Natural Science Illustrators and lives in St. Paul, Minnesota.